God's Names

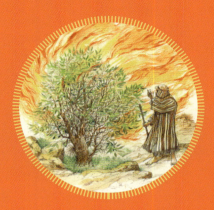

God's Names

BY SALLY MICHAEL

P&R
PUBLISHING
P.O. BOX 817 • PHILLIPSBURG • NEW JERSEY 08865-0817

Page design and typesetting by Dawn Premako

Printed in the United States of America

Library of Congress Cataloging-in-Publication Data

Michael, Sally, 1953-
  God's names / Sally Michael ; [illustrations by Fred Apps].
      p. cm.
  Includes bibliographical references.
  ISBN 978-1-59638-219-0 (pbk.)
  1. God (Christianity)--Name--Juvenile literature. I. Apps, Fred. II. Title.
  BT180.N2M53 2011
  231'.4--dc22
                                                    2010043771

Dedicated to my daughters,
son by marriage, and granddaughters.

Amy Jo—Beloved, Increasing Faithfulness
Kristina Lynne—Follower of Christ, Refreshing One
Gary Lee—Man of Loyalty, Gracious Spirit
Anna Hope—Gracious One, Hope
Katherine Joy—Pure, Joyful

May your names be remembered
by the Lord
forever.

And those who know your name
put their trust in you,
for you, O Lord, have not forsaken
those who seek you.
—Psalm 9:10

Contents

Preface 9

Introduction: How to Use This Book 10

Pronunciation Guide 14

1. Names, Names, Names 16

2. Elohim: Strong Creator 20

3. Jehovah, Yahweh, I AM: Self-Existent, Unchanging 24

4. El Shaddai: God Almighty 28

5. El Elyon: The Most High 32

6. El Kana: Jealous God 36

7. Jehovah-El Emeth: The LORD God of Truth 40

8. Adonai: Lord 44

9. El Roi: The God Who Sees 48

10. Jehovah-Shammah: The LORD Is There 52

11. A Strong Tower 56

12. Jehovah-Sabaoth: The LORD of Hosts 60

13. Jehovah-Jireh: The LORD Will Provide 64

14. Jehovah-Or: The LORD Is Light 68

15. Jehovah-Shalom: The LORD Is Peace 72

16. Judge of the Whole Earth 76

17. Jehovah-Maginnenu: The LORD Our Defense 80

18. Jehovah-Rohi: The LORD My Shepherd 84

19. Father 88

20. Lamb of God, Savior 92

21. Messiah, Christ 96

22. Salvation in No Other Name 100

23. Helper 104

24. Coming King 108

25. Overcomer 112

26. Knowing God's Name and Trusting Him 116

Preface

For our heart is glad in him, because we trust in his holy name.
—Psalm 33:21

The fruit of trusting in God is a "glad heart." Here is the pathway to true joy. To those of us who have walked with the Lord for a season, He has repeatedly proved that He is worthy of our admiration and trust. He has sustained our joy in the ordinary days and in unanticipated trials as we look forward to the *joy that is set before us*.

But our children may not know the Lord, or may just be beginning their walk with Him. They have not yet learned the unfathomable trustworthiness of God. Nor have they seen the glory of His unequaled character. Their tentative steps can be strengthened through our teaching of who God is, and through the experience of looking to God to show them that He is true to what He says about Himself.

You have before you a mini-primer on the character of God as revealed by His names. It is meant to be an interactive dialogue between adult and child as you discover God's character together. It is also intended to serve as a springboard for trusting God in everyday experiences as truth is applied in real life.

This book is a resource, but you, the parent, must focus your child's eyes on God by looking to Him daily, giving your son or daughter an example of dependence on God. You must model your own belief that God's name can be trusted and that He is worthy of our love and praise.

May the Lord bless your time together as you focus on God's names, and may your name and your children's names be remembered by the Lord forever.

Introduction
How to Use This Book

This book was written to give parents an opportunity to present solid truth to their children and to encourage real-life application of the truth.

Relational

Children receive more encouragement to learn when truth is presented by a trusted individual. Your positive, relational parent-child commitment will be a real benefit when you sit down together to read this book. Your time together over the Word should be positive, affirming, and loving.

Interactive

There is a greater impact when an individual discovers truth, instead of just hearing it presented. Many questions have been incorporated into the text of this book to encourage your child to wonder and think critically. The process of discovery will be circumvented if you don't give your child adequate time to think and respond. After asking a question, wait for a response. If your child has difficulty, ask the question a different way or give a few hints.

Questions and responses can be springboards for more questions and discovery as you interact with your child's mind and heart. The Holy Spirit is the real teacher, so depend on Him to give both you and your child thoughts and truths to explore together, and to bring the necessary understanding. Take the time to work through each story at a leisurely pace—giving time for interaction and further dialogue. The goal should be to get the material into the child, not just to get the child through the material.

Understandable

These stories have been written with attention given to explaining difficult or potentially new concepts. Some of these concepts may take time for your child to digest. Allow your child to ponder new truths. Read the story more than once, allowing the truth to be better understood and integrated to your child's theological framework. At times, have your child read parts of the lesson, giving an opportunity for visual learning.

Because vocabulary can be child-specific, define the particular words foreign to your child. Retell difficult sections in familiar wording, and ask questions to be sure your child understands the truth being taught.

Theological

More than just acquainting your child with the names of God, this book is building a biblical theology beneath your child. As your child begins to correctly understand who God is and how He interacts with the world, he or she won't just have a vague notion of God, but will be able to relate to the God of the Bible.

Because the Word of God has convicting and converting power, Bible texts are quoted word-for-word in some parts. Some of these verses may be beyond the child's understanding, so you may need to explain unfamiliar words or thoughts. Even though clear comprehension may be difficult, hearing the Word itself is a means the Holy Spirit can use to encourage faith in your child (Romans 10:17). Do not minimize the effectual influence of God's Word in the tender souls of children.

Since the Word of God is living and active, allow the child to read the Bible verses as much as possible. Also, encourage your child to memorize some of the verses so that he or she can meditate on them at other times.

The gospel is presented numerous times throughout the book. Use this as an opportunity to share God's work of grace in your life, and to converse with your child about his or her spiritual condition. Be careful not to confuse spiritual interest with converting faith and give premature assurances to your child. Fan the flames of gospel-inspired conviction and tenderness toward the sacrificial love of Jesus without prematurely encouraging your child to pray "the sinner's prayer."[1]

Application

Understanding the truth is essential, but insufficient. Truth must also be embraced in the heart and acted upon in daily life. Often, children cannot make the connection between a biblical truth and real-life application, so you, the parent, must help bridge the gap.

Consider the following quotation by D. Martyn Lloyd-Jones:

> We must always put things in the right order, and it is Truth first. . . . The heart is always to be influenced through the understanding—the mind, then the heart, then the will. . . . But God forbid that anyone should think that it ends with the intellect. It starts there, but it goes on. It then moves the heart and finally the man yields his will. He obeys, not grudgingly or unwillingly, but with the whole heart. The Christian life is a glorious perfect life that takes up and captivates the entire personality.[2]

Spend a few days or even a week on each name. Reread the story, discuss the truths, and follow the suggestions in the "Learning to Trust God" section. Most importantly, help your child to see that God is who He says He is, and to act in response to the truth. Point out God's involvement in daily life and thank Him for being true to His name.

---

1. Some excellent resources for parents regarding the salvation of children can be found at www.childrendesiring god.org. Resources include a booklet, *Helping Children Understand the Gospel*; and two seminars from the 2007 conference, " 'How Great a Salvation': Leading Children to a Solid Faith" and "Presenting the Gospel to Children."

2. D. Martyn Lloyd-Jones, *Spiritual Depression* (Grand Rapids: Eerdmans, 1965), 61–62.

Prayer

Ultimately, our efforts are effective only if the Holy Spirit breathes on our teaching and quickens it to the heart. Pray not only before going through the stories, but also in the succeeding days, that your child would see God's character and respond in faith to Him.

Note: We are using the concept of "name" loosely to refer to a name, title, or description.

Note: Although most scholars today prefer the translation *Yahweh* rather than *Jehovah* for the Divine Name, we are choosing to use *Jehovah* because this was more common during earlier times in the church's history. *Jehovah* is used in numerous hymns and has attained a long-standing place in our worship vocabulary. We do refer to both translations, but because of popular usage, *Jehovah* has been used in the compound names (e.g., *Jehovah-Shalom*) as well. For further discussion of this, reference: Geerhardus Vos, *Biblical Theology* (Carlisle, PA: Banner of Truth, 1996), 114–15.

Pronunciation Guide

Elohim (ĕl ō **hēm**)
Jehovah, Yahweh (jĕ **hō** vŭ; **yä** wā)
El Shaddai (ĕl shă **dī**)
El Elyon (ĕl ĕl **yŏn**)
El Kana (ĕl kä **nä**)
Jehovah-El Emeth (jĕ **hō** vŭ ĕl ĕ **mĕt**)
Adonai (ă dō **nī**)
El Roi (ĕl rō **ē**)
Jehovah-Shammah (jĕ **hō** vŭ shä **mä**)
Jehovah Sabaoth (jĕ **hō** vŭ să bā **ŏt**)
Jehovah-Jireh (jĕ **hō** vŭ jī **rŭ**)
Jehovah-Or (jĕ **hō** vŭ **or**)
Jehovah-Shalom (jĕ **hō** vŭ shä **lōm**)
Jehovah-Maginnenu (jĕ **hō** vŭ mä gĭ nĕ **new**)
Jehovah-Rohi (jĕ **hō** vŭ   **rō** hē)

ā = long a, as in "apron"	
ă = short a, as in "apple"	
ä = as in "father"	
ē = long e, as in "see"	
ĕ = short e, as in "egg"	
ī = long i, as in "ice"	
ō = long o, as in "open"	
ŏ = short o, as in "oxen"	
ŭ = short u, as in "umbrella"	

Stressed syllables are in **bold** type.

Note: Most Hebrew words put the stress on the last syllable (e.g., not El **KA** na, but El ka **NA**). Two exceptions in this list include "Jehovah," which has the stress on the second syllable, and "Rohi," which has the stress on the first syllable.

Names, Names, Names

How many names do you have? Let's find out! There's your first name. First names are names such as Sam, Ruth, Shannon, and Carlos. What is your first name?

Then there is your last name, which tells what family you are a part of—Nelson, Steward, Garcia, or Kasahara. What is your last name?

Some people also have a middle name. Do you?

But you have more names than this. Other names are called "titles"—like "son," or "daughter," or "sister." Does your family use those name-titles for you? Does Dad ever call you "Son"? Do your brothers or sisters ever call you "Sis" or "Bro"? Maybe you have even gotten a letter calling you "Mr." or "Miss."

Then there are the fun names! They are the special names that people who love you call you—"Sweetie" or "Pumpkin" or "Buster." These are called "nicknames."

Some nicknames are just a shorter way of saying your name—like using "Will" for "William." Other nicknames show something about you—like calling someone with red hair "Red," or calling someone "Speedy" because he runs really fast. Do you have any nicknames?

Usually a nickname describes you, or reminds you of something that happened to you, or says something about the kind of person you are. If you won a race, someone might give you the nickname "Champ"—short for "Champion." If you are smart, you might be called "The Brain."

To have ten names would be a lot! How many names do you have? Let's count them.

Sometimes there is a special reason that we have the first or middle name we have. Maybe you are named after someone who is loved by your parents—a grandfather, or an aunt or uncle. Sometimes there are clever reasons for choosing a name. If Mr. Joel and Mrs. Jackie chose "J" names for their children—Julia and Jesse—we could call them the "J"s!

Sometimes parents choose names with meanings because they want their children to grow up to be like the meaning of the names—such as Anna Hope and Katherine Joy. "Christina" means "follower of Christ," so parents might choose that name because they pray that their daughter would follow Jesus.

Why do you think your name was chosen for you?

Many names in the Bible mean something. "Eve" means "the mother of all living things." Why do you think she was named that?

God changed Abram's name to "Abraham," which means "father of a multitude of nations." The name "Abraham" showed God's plan for Abram's life. Jesus

changed Simon Peter's name to "Peter," which means "rock." Peter was not always strong like a rock. Can you think of some times when he was not like a rock? But Jesus changed Peter into a strong, rocklike man who was not afraid to preach about Jesus even when he was put in jail for his preaching.

Now, here is a very hard question. How many names do you think God has?

20 names? No, not enough!

50 names? Still not enough!

How about 100 names . . . this is STILL NOT ENOUGH!

The one true God of the Bible has MORE THAN 200 names![1] And if you were to count all the names, titles, and nicknames of God in the Bible, there are more than 700 names!

Wow!

Why do you think God has so many names?

Remember that a name in the Bible tells something about the person. God is so big . . . so GREAT, SO WONDERFUL, that it takes more than 700 names to tell what He is like! All His names have meanings—wonderful meanings that show how big and great and wonderful God is.

The Bible says, "And those who know your name put their trust in you" (Psalm 9:10).

Why do you think that knowing God's names will help you to trust Him—to know that He is strong and good and in control of all things, and able to take care of the whole world and everyone in it?

Would you like to learn some of these wonderful names of God? In this book we will learn only a small number of the many names of God, but every name we learn will tell us a little more about who God is and what He is like.

1. While God is called by many names in the Bible, He gives a special significance to the name Yahweh/Jehovah, often translated as "the Lord" (see Exodus 6:3).

Little by little by little, you will see how big and how great and HOW WONDERFUL GOD IS.

LEARNING TO TRUST GOD

✤ Look up Psalm 9:10 in your Bible. Read the whole verse and talk about it with your mom or dad.

✤ Ask God to help you to trust Him. Only God can give you a trusting heart. Ask God to help you to look for Him—to see every day that He is real and strong and good and wonderful.

✤ *Activity:* Find out why your name was chosen for you, and what your name means. Make a name card with your name and its meaning.

Elohim (ĕl ō hēm)
Strong Creator

The Bible shows us, little by little, name by name, who God is. It starts with the very first verse. Can you say the first verse in the Bible?

If you said Genesis 1:1, "In the beginning, God created the heavens and the earth," then you are right. The very first verse in the Bible tells us one of God's names: Elohim. "Elohim" is the name the Bible uses when it tells us about God creating the heavens and the earth and everything in them. In English, we say "God," but the Old Testament was written in the Hebrew language, and the Hebrew word for God is "Elohim." Can you say "Elohim"?

The very first thing we learn about God in the Bible is that He is the Creator and He made the whole world. Some people don't believe that God made the world, but the Bible is very clear that God is the Creator. *In the beginning, Elohim created the heavens and the earth.* The story of the creation of the world shows us that God, Elohim, is a strong, mighty, powerful Creator.

Let's try an experiment. Cut up ten small pieces of paper and number them 1–10. Put them in a paper lunch bag. Have your mom or dad help you blow up the bag like a balloon and twist the top. Then shake the bag. Did you shake it well? Now pop the bag by hitting it with your hand—maybe Mom or Dad can help you. Did it make a big BANG?

Dump out the paper numbers. Are the numbers in a nice straight line? Are they all right-side-up? Are the numbers in order from 1 to 10? How will the numbers get in order? Right, only if someone puts them in order. Order does not happen by itself.

Our world is like that, too. Someone had to create the world and put it in order. The trees didn't just fall into the ground with the roots going down. Someone had to put the stars in the sky and the mountains on the ground—instead of the other way around. That Someone is God, Elohim, Strong Creator.

Think about the trees. Are the leaves ever on the inside? No, they are always on the outside. Think about how flowers grow. Every flower has a stem. The stem has leaves. The petals grow out of the center of the flower. Do petals ever grow out of the ground? No, flowers follow a pattern—stem in the ground, leaves on the stem, petals from the center. Do patterns happen all by themselves? Who made the pattern for flowers? It was God, Elohim, the strong, mighty, powerful Creator.

When you made your numbers, you used paper. Did you make the paper? No, you used something that was already made. You didn't make the paper . . . or the

tree the paper was made from . . . or the sun that made the tree grow . . . or the seed that grew into a tree. You needed all these things to make your paper numbers.

Who made all the things the world is made from? It had to be Someone strong and mighty and powerful. Elohim, the Strong Creator, made the world and everything in it out of nothing! God just spoke and the world was created by His words. God is Elohim, the Strong Creator. No one helped God. He created the world by Himself. This is what God said about creating the world:

> I am the LORD, who made all things,
>> who alone stretched out the heavens,
>> who spread out the earth by myself. (Isaiah 44:24)

God did not need any help. He is Elohim, Strong Creator.

How many sandwiches could you make for your family? Could you make 10 sandwiches? Could you make 50? Could you make 500? Why couldn't you make 500? Yes, you would get too tired, and you would run out of bread and other things for your sandwiches.

But God never gets tired, and He never runs out of things. Remember, He is Elohim, strong, mighty, powerful Creator. God didn't make one bug or 50 bugs or even 500 bugs . . . God made MILLIONS of bugs! We don't even really know how many bugs God made, because we keep finding bugs we didn't know about. Only a strong, mighty, powerful Creator could make so many bugs. Only Elohim! Our God, Elohim, never gets stuck—He doesn't run out of "bug material." He never runs out of energy. He never runs out of ideas!

We haven't even discovered all that God has created. Think about beetles. How many different kinds of beetles have you seen? We aren't even sure how many kinds of beetles there are, because we are still finding more of God's beetles. Some say 300,000. Others say 350,000. How do you know when man has found all the kinds of beetles? But Elohim knows because He made every single one of them.

Don't you think God must have enjoyed making all those kinds of beetles—each one a beetle, but each one different?

"Elohim" is God. And God is a strong, mighty, powerful Creator. When we look at God's creation, our hearts should say, "God, you are great! You are Elohim, Strong Creator." We should say, like Jeremiah:

Ah, Lord GOD! It is you who have made the heavens and the earth by your great power and by your outstretched arm! Nothing is too hard for you. (Jeremiah 32:17)

LEARNING TO TRUST GOD

✛ Read Jeremiah 32:17 again. Ask God to give you a heart like Jeremiah's that knows nothing is too hard for God.

✛ Sing a worship song or hymn about the greatness of God.

✛ *Activity:* Discover God's world. Take a hike with your family. Look at the patterns in the world. Try to count the number of different things you find. Remind yourself of Jeremiah 32:17.

Jehovah, Yahweh, I AM
(jĕ hō vŭ; yä wā)
Self-Existent, Unchanging

Are you ready to learn a big word? First, let's learn to say the word.

> egg (like what you eat with toast)
> ziss (like "hiss" but with a z)
> tent (like what you use when camping)

Can you say "egg ziss tent"? This is what the word looks like: existent.

But what does "existent" mean? This is really important because this next name for God means He is "self-existent and unchanging." The name is YHWH, which is a name we can't say. We can only spell out the letters. This is God's most special name.

If you want to copy a page, you can use a copy machine. But in Bible times, men copying the Bible had to write every word by hand. When they got to the name of God, they would skip it and leave a blank space. Later they would write God's name with a special "God pen." Why do you think they used a special pen for God's name?

God's name was so precious, so special that they used a special pen not used for anything else. God's personal name, YHWH, was so special that they would not even say it. So it was written YHWH, which cannot be spoken. Much later, extra letters were added to make it "Yahweh" in Hebrew or "Jehovah" in Latin. In your English Bible, it looks like this: LORD.

"Yahweh" or "Jehovah" means "I AM." Let's see what "I AM" means.

Do you remember the story of Moses and the burning bush? What was strange about that burning bush?

This bush burned and burned, but it never burned up. If you burn a piece of wood, does it burn forever? No, the fire burns out because the wood burns up and there is nothing left to burn. But this bush kept burning and did not burn up. God used the burning, never-burned-out bush to show Moses something about Himself—that He is "self-existent and unchanging."

God spoke to Moses from the burning bush. He said He knew about the Hebrew people who were slaves in Egypt. And God said He would set them free. God told Moses to bring His people out of Egypt.

But Moses had a problem. He didn't know God's name. This is what he said to God:

Then Moses said to God, "If I come to the people of Israel and say to them, 'The God of your fathers has sent me to you,' and they ask me, 'What is his name?' what shall I say to them?" God said to Moses, "I AM WHO I AM." And he said, "Say this to the people of Israel, 'I AM has sent me to you.'" God also said to Moses, "Say this to the people of Israel, 'The LORD, the God of your fathers, the God of Abraham, the God of Isaac, and the God of Jacob, has sent me to you.' This is my name forever." (Exodus 3:13–15)

The LORD, Yahweh, Jehovah said to Moses, "I AM. . . . This is my name forever." What does the name "I AM" mean?

It means God is real. He is not made up. He is alive and lives forever. Just as the bush was never burned up, God never wears out. He never gets tired or needs to sleep. God never gets used up. And He never dies.

Here is where our big word comes in. "Existent" means "real" or "living now." God is "*self*-existent." That means He is living without the help of anything else— all by Himself. He doesn't need anything, not air to breathe, or sleep to make Him strong. He doesn't need a mom or a dad, doctors or policemen. He doesn't need any help. He DOESN'T NEED ANYTHING TO EXIST. He is "self-existent."

This is what the book of Acts says about God, who is self-existent and who doesn't need anything:

The God who made the world and everything in it, being Lord of heaven and earth, does not live in temples made by man, nor is he served by human hands, as though he needed anything, since he himself gives to all mankind life and breath and everything. (Acts 17:24–25)

God, Elohim, the Strong Creator, who made everything, is Jehovah, I AM, who *doesn't need anything*. Instead, he *gives us everything!*

God gives us air, food, water, sleep, parents. Everything we have comes from God, who doesn't need anything.

Everything we have gets used up or worn out. Everyone we know will die someday. But not God. He never gets worn out. He is always strong, always alive, always in charge of the world He made. He NEVER CHANGES. He is always God, Elohim, Strong Creator. He is always Yahweh, Jehovah, I AM—the self-existent God, who does not need anything and never changes. He is God and He is great.

> Of old you laid the foundation of the earth,
>   and the heavens are the work of your hands.
> They will perish, but you will remain;
>   they will all wear out like a garment.
> You will change them like a robe, and they will pass away,
>   but you are the same, and your years have no end. (Psalm 102:25–27)

LEARNING TO TRUST GOD

✢ Read Romans 11:34–36. How do these verses end? Why is it right for us to praise God?

✢ Talk about why we can trust a God who doesn't need anything and never changes.

✢ Praise Jehovah for being alive and strong, and never needing anything and never changing. Ask Him to help you to trust Him.

✢ *Activity:* Make a large poster of the names of God, leaving room to add many more names as you learn them. Decorate the names. What did you need to create your poster? Remember that God, Elohim, created the world from *nothing* and that God, Jehovah, doesn't ever need *anything*.

El Shaddai (ĕl shă dī)
God Almighty

If someone *says* he can draw really well, would you believe him? Maybe he's teasing, or not telling the truth. Maybe he thinks he can draw better than he really can.

But if he draws a picture and *shows* you that he can draw really well, then you *know* he can do it. After he proves he isn't teasing, doesn't lie, and understands what he can do, you know you can *trust* him.

All through the Bible, God has shown that He can be trusted. He has proved that He is God Almighty.

God told Abram to leave his home and family, and travel far away to another country. God said that He would make from Abram a great new family of people. Abram believed and obeyed God, and there was plenty of time to have children, grandchildren, and great-grandchildren.

Abram waited and waited. But God did not give him a son. Abram and his wife Sarai waited for years. But still they had no children.

God told him again, "Abram, I will make a great new family of people from you. I will give you a lot of land and more people in your family than you can count." Abram *trusted* God. He believed that God would keep His promise. So he waited and waited again for years. But still they had no children.

Did God forget His promise? Was God teasing or not telling the truth? Or was God not able to give Abram a great big family?

Abram and Sarai got older. Abram talked to God about having a child. Would his servant be the person to start Abram's family, since he did not have a son? No. God *told* Abram that he would have his own son. He would have as many people in his family as there are stars in the sky. Abram believed God and waited. He waited so long that he became an old man, but still they had no children.

Maybe Abram should not have a baby with Sarai, his wife. Maybe Sarai's servant, Hagar, should have Abram's child. Abram had waited so long. Soon he would be too old to have a child. So Abram had a son with Hagar, which was wrong. But God did not want to make Abram's family from Hagar's son. God would make Abram wait even longer. Would Abram keep believing God's promise?

Abram waited some more. When he was 99, and too old to have children, God told Abram about His promise again. This time God changed Abram's name to "Abraham," which means "father of many nations." He changed Sarai's name to "Sarah." God also told Abram another of His own many names—El Shaddai, or God Almighty. This is what El Shaddai, God Almighty, said to Abram:

I am God Almighty; walk before me, and be blameless, that I may make my covenant between me and you, and may multiply you greatly. (Genesis 17:1–2)

God *told* Abram that He is God Almighty—He has

all power, nothing is too hard for Him, He can do all things, and He is all-sufficient. But now He would also *show* Abram that He is El Shaddai, God Almighty. When Abraham was 100 and Sarah was 90, God gave them their very own son, Isaac. Abraham and Sarah were very old—too old to have a child. But God is El Shaddai, God Almighty, and nothing is too hard for our Mighty God. He can even make old people have babies!

Is anything too hard for the Lord? (Genesis 18:14)

No! All through the Bible, God shows us that He is El Shaddai, God Almighty. Nothing is too hard for Him. He is all-powerful. He can do all things. He can flood the earth with water and dry it up again, open a path through the sea for His people and close it on their enemies, send a big fish to save a man, and use a boy's lunch to feed thousands. He can make blind eyes see, bring the dead back to life, and quiet a storm. God can do anything! He is El Shaddai, God Almighty! Nothing is too hard for Him!

We can *trust* God, who has *told* us and *shown* us that He is El Shaddai. He has proved over and over that nothing is too hard for Him. Moses wrote in the Bible:

O Lord God, you have only begun to show your servant your greatness and your mighty hand. For what god is there in heaven or on earth who can do such works and mighty acts as yours? (Deuteronomy 3:24)

What is the answer to the question, "What god is there in heaven or on earth who can do such works and mighty acts as yours?" There is no god like Elohim, the Creator of the whole world. Only Jehovah, Yahweh, I am needs nothing and never changes. Only El Shaddai, God Almighty, is the one true God who can do all things. How great is our God! Someday the whole world will *see* the greatness of El Shaddai, God Almighty.

LEARNING TO TRUST GOD

✤ Read Deuteronomy 3:24 again. What are some of God's mighty acts in the Bible? What are some ways God has shown your family that He is El Shaddai?

✤ Is there anything you are waiting for God to do? Ask God to help you to trust Him, even when you must wait a long time for Him to act.

✤ *Activity:* Ask someone who has been a Christian for many years to tell you about some of the mighty acts of God he has seen. Did he ever have to wait a long time for God to answer prayer or to keep His promise? What is one verse that helped him to trust God?

El Elyon (ĕl ĕl yŏn)
The Most High

——— ——— ——————

Which line takes up the MOST space? The last line is the MOST long and MOST thick, so it takes up the MOST space. Is there more than one most-long, most-thick line? Only one is the MOST. Being the MOST means it is the greatest.

God has a name that tells us He is the MOST. That name is "El Elyon." How is God the most? God is the MOST perfect, powerful, wise, kind, good, faithful, creative, generous, happy, patient . . . the list could go on and on. God is greater than anyone or anything. He is El Elyon, the Most High.

Could anyone make himself as great as God? The Bible tells about someone who tried.

The verses could be about a proud, evil king of Babylon, or they could be about Satan. Whoever it was, this is what Isaiah says:

You said in your heart,
    "I will ascend to heaven;
above the stars of God
    I will set my throne on high;
. . . .
I will ascend above the heights of the clouds;
    I will make myself like the Most High." (Isaiah 14:13–14)

"Ascend" means "to go up." Isaiah is writing about someone who thought he could go up to heaven and take God's throne. He thought he could be as great as God, and be like El Elyon, the Most High.

But no one can be like God. No one can take His throne and be the greatest king. There can be only one Most High—Yahweh, El Shaddai. No one rules over the world but Elohim, Strong Creator.

What happened to the one who tried to take God's throne? Isaiah said he was "cut to the ground . . . brought down to the far reaches of the pit" (Isaiah 14:15). The one who tried to be the most high became the most low. He was thrown down to the pit of death.

Can you think of some great people? You might think of a president such as George Washington, an inventor like airplane builders Orville and Wilbur Wright, a writer like Dr. Seuss, or a ruler like King David. God is better and greater than anyone else. God is the best. He is the Most High. He is the King of Kings!

Kings are in charge of people. They make laws or rules. They decide big things like whether there will be a war, and they decide little things like what to name a city. Some kings are good and do what is good for their people. Some are bad and do what is good for themselves. But God is the BEST King—the MOST patient, good, wise, loving, and faithful King. He always does what is best for His people. And because He is the MOST powerful, He is always able to do what He wants. God is El Shaddai, God Almighty. Nothing is too hard for Him.

The greatest kings in the world are not greater than God. A king rules over his own country—like Spain or Sweden. But God is the "King of all the earth." He is the King of all kings! He is the Most High King over every king who ever lived.

A long time ago, there was a king who thought he was pretty great. He thought he ruled over a great country. He proudly looked around at his kingdom from the roof of his palace and said:

> Is not this great Babylon, which I have built by my mighty power as a royal residence and for the glory of my majesty? (Daniel 4:30)

He thought he was great and powerful. He did not think about God, El Elyon, the Most High, who had helped him build a great city. He did not thank God for making him a king, or praise God for being so great. He did not think about being a little king of Babylon and God being the great King of the whole earth. He thought "King Nebuchadnezzar" was a great name for a great king. He did not think about El Elyon, the Most High, being a greater name for the greatest King.

So God showed him how very little and unimportant he was. God took away King Nebuchadnezzar's good mind. He not only forgot he was a king, but even forgot he was a man! He ate grass, lived with the animals, and acted like an animal for a very long time—until God made his mind better, and then he knew that the Most High God rules the whole world. Then the little king saw that God is the greatest King, who rules forever, does whatever He wants, cannot be stopped by anyone, and always does what is good and right.

God is a great King! He is the King of all kings—the greatest King, the Most High, El Elyon. Does this make you happy? Are you glad God is the Most High?

> Clap your hands, all peoples!
>> Shout to God with loud songs of joy!
> For the Lord, the Most High, is to be feared,
>> a great king over all the earth. (Psalm 47:1–2)

LEARNING TO TRUST GOD

✛ Make up a song for Psalm 47:1–2 and sing it with your family. Clap your hands as you sing! It is a happy thing that God is the Most High, because He is a King who always does what is good and right.

✛ What makes you sad, or scared, or angry? Do you know that God rules over those things? They are not bigger or greater than He is. Pray and thank God that He is the Most High. Tell Him what makes you sad, scared, or angry. Ask Him to help you to trust Him, and to remind you that He is El Elyon, the Most High.

✛ *Activity:* Who can you tell that God is the Most High, the King of all kings? Write a note, make a card, record a song, draw a picture or a poster, or make a video to tell about El Elyon.

El Kana (ĕl kä nä)
Jealous God

The Bible tells us about two people who were known as Jesus' friends. They walked, ate, and talked with Jesus, but were very different from each other. One was Mary, the sister of Lazarus. She had something that cost a lot of money—even more than a car would cost today. Do you know what Mary had that cost so much?

It was a bottle of perfume. Very, very expensive perfume! What would Mary do with perfume that cost so much? Because Mary loved Jesus very much, she broke the bottle and poured the perfume over Jesus' head. She used the perfume to wash Jesus' feet—feet that walked from town to town on dusty roads collecting dirt through the holes in Jesus' sandals, feet that would soon be nailed to a cross for Mary.

The smell of the perfume filled the house, and love for Jesus filled Mary's heart. She knew that Jesus, just like the Father, was God and that He was almighty—even able to raise her brother from the dead. Jesus was "the most high" in Mary's heart. He was the King of Kings, more important than anyone else. Mary served Jesus by doing the dirty job of washing His feet. And then she dried His feet with her hair.

So much money poured out on Jesus! It made Mary happy to do it, because she loved Jesus most of all.

The other person was Judas. He was not like Mary. He did not think about the greatness of Jesus—a King so great, who owned the whole world and all the perfume in it, the One who ruled over all things and did not need anything. Jesus was not "most high" in Judas's heart.

So much money poured out on Jesus! It made Judas angry and upset, because he loved money more than he loved Jesus. In Judas's heart, Jesus was not God.

Money was Judas's god. He wanted it, thought about it, and even stole it. Judas loved money.

To want, think about, and love something most of all, and do anything to get it, is called "worship." To worship something or someone is to make it most important or "most high" in our hearts. People can worship money, friends, being in charge, having fun, or anything else. But the Bible says that only God should be "most high" in our hearts. Nothing else should take God's place and be god to us. Do you remember these words from the Ten Commandments?

You shall have no other gods before me. (Exodus 20:3)

The name of God that reminds us of this is "El Kana." It means "jealous." The Bible tells us about this name:

You shall worship no other god, for the Lord, whose name is Jealous, is a jealous God. (Exodus 34:14)

We usually think about jealousy as being unhappy because someone has something we don't have, or being upset because someone is better at something than we are. But that isn't what the Bible means when it says that God is "jealous." God cannot be upset because someone has something He doesn't have—God owns everything in the whole world. No one can be better at something than God is, because God is the best at everything good. So God is not unhappy or jealous in that way.

When the Bible talks about God's being "jealous," it means that God wants us to love Him most of all. He alone is El Elyon, the Most High. He alone is to be most important—to have first place. He alone is the King of Kings, and God will not share His first place with anything or anyone. He is a "jealous God."

God showed us this in the Bible. The ark of God was a special box covered with gold. It held the tablets on which the Ten Commandments were written, Aaron's rod, and the special bread called "manna" that God had given His people to eat in the desert. The ark reminded the people that God was with them and that He is great.

But the enemies of Israel took the ark. Where do you think they put it? They did not care about worshiping the one true God. They had many gods—gods who did not make the world and everything in it, but gods they made from stone, wood, and metal. One of their gods was Dagon, who looked like part man and part fish. They had a special house for Dagon, the man-fish god, and they put the ark of God right beside Dagon.

But God is a jealous God. To show the people that He will not share first place with anything or anyone, He made Dagon fall in front of the ark. The people still did not want to worship God alone as the one true God, so they put Dagon back in his place. What do you think the one true God, El Shaddai, God Almighty did about that? He made Dagon fall again. And this time his head and both his hands broke off! What do you think God was showing the people?

God is El Elyon, the Most High. He is El Kana, Jealous God, who will not be second to anyone or anything. He alone should have first place in our hearts.

LEARNING TO TRUST GOD

✢ Read about Jesus, Mary, and the perfume in John 12:1–7. Would you like to be more like Mary or like Judas? Pray and ask God to give you a heart like Mary's—a heart that loves Jesus most of all.

✢ Talk to your mom or dad about why it is right that God is El Kana, Jealous God. Why is it good for us that God is El Kana, Jealous God?

✢ *Activity:* Mary showed great love for Jesus in happily giving Him such an expensive gift. What could you do with a happy heart to show that Jesus should be loved most of all? Talk about your ideas with your mom or dad, and ask Jesus to give you a happy heart to do them.

Jehovah-El Emeth
(jĕ hō vŭ ĕl ĕ mĕt)
The LORD God of Truth

Let's have a quiz! What is the truth, and what is a lie?

> Cows have two ears. Truth? Or lie?
> Rocks are hard. Truth? Or lie?
> Horses have eight legs. Truth? Or lie?

How do you know that the last statement is a lie? You know because you have seen horses. You know they have four legs. Since you know the truth about horses, you know the lie is a lie. To catch lies, you must know the truth.

Here is the greatest truth in the whole world and one of God's many names: God is Jehovah-El Emeth, the LORD God of Truth. God *always* speaks the truth. He *never* lies. This is what the Bible, the truth that God has spoken, says:

> God is not man, that he should lie,
> or a son of man, that he should change his mind.
> Has he said, and will he not do it?
> Or has he spoken, and will he not fulfill it? (Numbers 23:19)

God is Jehovah-El Emeth, the LORD God of Truth. Every word He speaks is the truth, and He does everything He says He will do.

Now, how do we know this is true?

Do you remember what God told Adam in the garden of Eden about the Tree of Knowledge of Good and Evil? What did He say would happen if Adam ate the fruit of that tree? Here are God's very words from the Bible:

And the LORD God commanded the man, saying, "You may surely eat of every tree of the garden, but of the tree of the knowledge of good and evil you shall not eat, for in the day that you eat of it you shall surely die." (Genesis 2:16–17)

But what did Satan, who came as a serpent, say to Eve? These are his very words:

You will not surely die. (Genesis 3:4)

Both of these statements can't be true. God said one thing—"You *will* surely die"—and Satan said another, "You *will not* surely die." Which was true? Is God really Jehovah-El Emeth, the LORD God of Truth?

Did Eve believe God or Satan? Who did Adam obey? What happened after Eve, and then Adam, followed Satan's lie instead of God's truth and ate the fruit? Are Adam and Eve still alive today? Do people die? Death came into the world, just as God said it would.

Who is the truth-teller, God or Satan? Who is the liar? God is Jehovah-El Emeth, the LORD God of Truth.

Every word of God proves true. (Proverbs 30:5)

Every single word God speaks is the truth. But this is what the Bible says about Satan:

He was a murderer from the beginning, and has nothing to do with the truth, because there is no truth in him. When he lies, he speaks out of his own character, for he is a liar and the father of lies. (John 8:44)

There is one truth, God's truth found in the Bible. But there are many lies. All those lies are against Jehovah-El Emeth, the LORD God of Truth. Lies are everywhere. Some are found in books, in movies, on bumper stickers and posters, on the radio . . . from friends and other people . . . everywhere. Lies hurt. God hates lies.

How do you know when you hear a lie? You must know the truth. Truth is found in Jehovah-El Emeth, the LORD God of Truth. The Bible is His Word, and every word of His is true.

Anything that does not agree with the Bible is not the truth. It is a lie. Only by following the truth can we live right. Only by knowing Jehovah-El Emeth, the LORD God of Truth, can we find real joy. Only Jesus can protect us from the lies of this world.

Every word of God proves true;

    he is a shield to those who take refuge in him. (Proverbs 30:5)

LEARNING TO TRUST GOD

✛ Read the story of the fall in Genesis 3. What sad things happened because of following a lie?

✛ Talk to your mom or dad about God being a shield. How do God and His Word "shield" us from lies? Are you learning God's truth in the Bible? Do you love the Bible? Pray and ask God to give you a love for the truth and a hatred of lies.

✛ *Activity:* Look for lies. Make a booklet of the lies you find. What truths are these lies against? With Mom or Dad's help, burn the booklet to show that lies are wrong and hurtful, and we should hate them. Memorize Proverbs 30:5 and thank God for His Word of Truth, the Bible.

Adonai (ă dō nī)
Lord

Wouldn't it be strange if you were drawing a tree, and the crayon jumped out of your hand and said, "I don't want to draw a tree! I want to draw a boat!" It would be VERY strange because crayons don't talk. But it would also be strange because you are the owner of the crayon. You are in charge, and you get to decide what it will draw.

The Bible uses the same kind of strange thing to show how foolish and wrong it is to think we should be in charge instead of God. Here is what the Bible says:

> Woe to him who strives with him who formed him,
>   a pot among earthen pots!
> Does the clay say to him who forms it, "What are you making?"
>   or "Your work has no handles"? (Isaiah 45:9)

Clay doesn't get to decide what kind of pot is made with it. It doesn't get to say, "You should give me handles!" The owner of the clay decides everything about the pot.

God made us and the whole world, so He owns everything. He gets to decide what to do with everything in His world. "Lord" is a title that shows someone is the owner of something. The Hebrew way of saying "Lord" is "Adonai."

God is Adonai, Lord or owner of everything. God is a good owner. He loves us and gives us what we need. He takes care of us and the world.

If God is the owner of us and all things, should we be like the crayon or the pot and say, "No, don't do this" to God? Should we be like Jonah, who went *away* from Nineveh when God told him to go *to* Nineveh? Or should we be like Mary? She said:

Behold, I am the servant of the Lord; let it be to me according to your word. (Luke 1:38)

Mary understood that God is Adonai, the Lord, and that she was His servant to do whatever He said.

Sometimes we don't feel like obeying God. Sometimes what He tells us to do is hard, or doesn't seem like a good idea to us. But we are not Adonai, the Lord. God is. He is always right and always good. He is El Elyon, the Most High who rules the whole world. He is Jehovah-El Emeth, the Lord God of Truth, so He is never wrong.

No matter how we feel or what we think, we must obey Adonai. We need to be like Simon. Simon and the other fishermen had been fishing all night and were washing their nets. They were tired and maybe hungry. And they were probably a little upset, because even though they had worked hard, they had not caught any fish.

Jesus got into Simon's boat and taught the people.

And when he had finished speaking, he said to Simon, "Put out into the deep and let down your nets for a catch." (Luke 5:4)

Did Jesus make a mistake? It was not the time for fishing. The fishermen were tired, and there weren't any fish. How would Simon answer Jesus?

And Simon answered, "Master, we toiled all night and took nothing!" (Luke 5:5)

Simon knew how to catch fish. He knew it was not the time for fishing. He and the other fishermen were tired. But what did he call Jesus?

He called Jesus "Master." A master is an owner. Servants do what masters tell them to do. Jesus is the Master. Just like the Father, He too is the Lord. He is Adonai. So this is what Simon said:

Master, we toiled all night and took nothing! But at your word I will let down the nets. (Luke 5:5)

"At your word." Simon knew Jesus was the Lord. Jesus was the owner of Simon and the other fishermen, the boat, fish, you and me . . . and the whole world. So Simon obeyed the word of Jesus, the Master.

Do you know what happened when Simon obeyed Jesus, rowed out to the deep water, and put down the nets? Jesus made fish swim into the nets! There were so many fish that the nets started to break! Simon knew that Jesus truly is the Master, the only owner of all things. Jesus is different from anyone else.

Do you know this about Jesus? Do you have a heart that says, "At your word . . . I will do what You say; I will do what is right even when I don't feel like it; I will follow Your laws even when others don't. Whatever You say, I will obey because You are Adonai, the Lord, and I am Your servant"?

LEARNING TO TRUST GOD

✤ Read about Simon and Jesus in Luke 5:1–11. Try to imagine what it was like to be Simon. How would you have answered Jesus?

✤ Do you obey those who are in charge of you? When you obey those in charge, you are actually obeying God. What does it say about your heart when you disobey? Are you loving God as Adonai, the Lord and Master? Pray for a heart that says, "I will obey your Word."

✤ *Activity:* Write the Ten Commandments from Exodus 20. Your mom or dad can help you. Talk about the rules or laws of El Elyon, the Most High, Adonai, the Lord who owns all things and is to be obeyed.

El Roi (ĕl rō ē)

The God Who Sees

What can you see right now? If you had a microscope, you could see really tiny things. With a telescope, you could see things far away. With a tiny camera, a doctor could even see inside your body.

But there are things no person can see. What can't you see?

You can't see another person's thoughts or feelings. You can't see tomorrow or next year. You can't see all the people who have ever lived, and those who haven't been born yet.

But God sees all these things. He is El Shaddai, God Almighty. He is also El Roi, the God Who Sees. The God who sees everyone, all the time, in every place. The God who sees everyone's thoughts and heart. The God who sees tomorrow, and next year, and all of time. The God who sees . . . and knows . . . and understands all things.

Hagar was Sarai's maid. Sarai gave her to Abram so that he could have a child. And then Sarai got angry. Angry at Hagar—and at Abram. So Abram told Sarai she could do whatever she wanted to do to Hagar.

Sarai was so mean to Hagar that Hagar ran away into the wilderness. Away from Sarai. Away from Abram—and everyone.

But Hagar was not alone. God knew all about Hagar, and He sent an angel to her. The angel told Hagar to go back to Sarai and to obey her. The angel gave her God's promise:

Behold, you are pregnant and shall bear a son. You shall call his name Ishmael, because the LORD has listened to your affliction. He shall be a wild donkey of a man, his hand against everyone and everyone's hand against him, and he shall dwell over against all his kinsmen. (Genesis 16:11–12)

God knew Hagar would have a child . . . a son. He knew what Ishmael would be like and what would happen to him. God saw inside Hagar's body to the baby. God saw tomorrow and the next year, and beyond. God saw the heart of Ishmael.

But God saw even more than this. He saw Hagar. He saw her thoughts and fears, her worries and feelings. He saw her loneliness and how she was treated by Sarai—He "listened to her affliction." God saw . . . and God understood. God saw Hagar with eyes of kindness and love, and He took care of her.

Hagar saw something, too. Hagar saw a little of who God really is.

So she called the name of the LORD who spoke to her, "You are a God of seeing," for she said, "Truly here I have seen him who looks after me." (Genesis 16:13)

How did Hagar describe God? When she called God "a God of seeing," she showed us another of His names.

God is El Roi, the God Who Sees. He is the God who sees everything and "looks after" everything.

The LORD is good to all,
and his mercy is over all that he has made. (Psalm 145:9)

God did not just make the world and leave it alone. He watches over the world and everyone in it. He knows about everything in the world and everything in your life. Nothing is too small for Him to notice. And nothing is too far away or too hidden for Him to see. He is El Roi, the God Who Sees.

Some people think God sees just so that He can know all the bad things we do—that He is always angry. God is angry at sin. But God is also full of love and kindness, and He understands our hurts, fears, and problems. He loves to help those who call on Him and trust Him.

The eyes of the LORD are toward the righteous
and his ears toward their cry.
The face of the LORD is against those who do evil,
to cut off the memory of them from the earth. (Psalm 34:15–16)

Do you want God to see and hear you with special love and kindness when you cry out to Him? Or do you want Him to turn His face away and be against you? El Roi, the God Who Sees, always looks with special love and kindness on those who know Him as Adonai, the Lord; who worship only Him, El Kana, Jealous God; who believe Jehovah-El Emeth, the LORD God of Truth; and who trust in Jesus as Savior.

LEARNING TO TRUST GOD

✢ Read about El Roi, the God Who Sees, in Genesis 16:1–16. Think about all the things God saw. Think about what Hagar learned about God. What does God see about you?

✢ Talk to your mom and dad about Psalm 34:15–16. Who are the righteous? Who are those who do evil? Is El Roi the same to both of them? How can you be righteous?

✢ *Activity:* God sent an angel to tell Hagar about Him. There are many people like Hagar, who are sad or sick, or have a big problem. You and your family could remind someone about El Roi, the God Who Sees, and who understands. You could remind someone of the truth that Jehovah-El Emeth tells us in His Word. And you could do something kind and loving for that person.

Jehovah-Shammah
(jĕ hō vŭ shä mä)
The Lord Is There

A little girl needed something from the basement. It was dark in the basement . . . and there were bugs. What do you think she asked her sister to do?

"Will you come with me?" she said. Why do you think she said that? Have you ever asked another person to be with you? When we are afraid, nervous, sad, or unsure of something new, it is nice to have another person with us.

El Roi, the God Who Sees, understands that it is hard to be alone sometimes—especially when we are afraid or sad. El Roi saw the Hebrew people in Egypt. He saw that they were slaves and Pharaoh treated them wrongly. He understood their pain.

God Almighty brought the Hebrew people out of Egypt and promised them a new land. There were two ways to get to the Promised Land. One way was through the land of the Philistines. They were great warrior fighters . . . and very scary . . . and they didn't like the Hebrews.

The other way was through the wilderness. But the wilderness had scary things, too—wild animals and poisonous snakes. And there were some things it didn't have much of—water and food. So that was scary, too.

God didn't make fun of the Hebrews for being afraid, or tell them that they were babies. He didn't get angry at them. He understood that they were weak and fearful.

Do you think God said, "Well, I got you out of Egypt. I'll see you in the Promised Land"? No, He didn't. He didn't leave them because He is Jehovah-Shammah, the Lord Is There. God is not far away; He is there with His people . . . all the time, no matter where they are.

God led the Hebrew people into the wilderness, away from the Philistines, and was with them day and night. He never left them.

And the LORD went before them by day in a pillar of cloud to lead them along the way, and by night in a pillar of fire to give them light, that they might travel by day and by night. The pillar of cloud by day and the pillar of fire by night did not depart from before the people. (Exodus 13:21–22)

God not only told the Hebrews He was with them. He also showed them by giving them a cloud and a fire. He knew they were weak and needed to see that He was with them. He even gave them a promise later when He brought them into the Promised Land:

Have I not commanded you? Be strong and courageous. Do not be frightened, and do not be dismayed, for the LORD your God is with you wherever you go. (Joshua 1:9)

If you are a child of God, God is with you wherever you go, too. No matter where you are, even when you think you are alone, God is still with you. He is with you in the dark, and in a new place. He is with His children when they are sad and when they are happy. He does not leave them when they do something wrong. He helps them do what is right.

Jehovah-Shammah is there with His people all the time. There is nowhere we can go that He does not go with us. Jonah tried to run away from God—but he couldn't! God is everywhere with His people, because He loves them.

Where shall I go from your Spirit?
    Or where shall I flee from your presence?
If I ascend to heaven, you are there!
    If I make my bed in Sheol, you are there!
If I take the wings of the morning
    and dwell in the uttermost parts of the sea,
even there your hand shall lead me,
    and your right hand shall hold me. (Psalm 139:7–10)

Thank You, God, for being Jehovah-Shammah, the God Who Is There. Thank You for never leaving us—anywhere, anytime, for any reason. You are good and You are faithful. Help me to trust and love You.

LEARNING TO TRUST GOD

✢ Talk with your family about times when you were glad someone else was with you. Why did it help that you were not alone? How does the help of that person compare with God's help?

✢ Make sure your poster has all the names of God you have learned. Pray with your family using God's many names. Remember to praise Him, thank Him, tell Him your needs, and ask His forgiveness for sin.

✢ *Activity:* Look through family pictures. Talk about how God was with you in every picture. How did He help your family? How did He show Himself as Elohim, Strong Creator; Yahweh, Self-Existent and Unchanging; El Shaddai, God Almighty; El Elyon, the Most High; El Kana, Jealous God; Jehovah-El Emeth, the Lord God of Truth; Adonai, Lord; El Roi, the God Who Sees; Jehovah-Shammah, the Lord Is There?

A Strong Tower

Imagine being outside during a big storm. There is booming thunder, jagged lightning, howling wind, and sheets of rain. You are soaked and cold. What would be your first thought?

You might think, "I need to get inside!" Would you want to be inside a tent? Of course not! How about a big, strong, stone tower? You would feel very safe and protected inside the tower. The rain could not get in, the wind could not blow it over, and the thunder wouldn't be as loud in the tower. Even the lightning wouldn't seem so bad.

The Bible says, **"The name of the LORD is a strong tower; the righteous man runs into it and is safe" (Proverbs 18:10).**

Just as a strong tower keeps you safe from storms, God's name keeps everyone safe who is trusting in Jesus. Does this mean that nothing will ever hurt God's children? No. It means that nothing will hurt God's children *forever*. Nothing can take their joy away *forever*.

When you run inside from a storm, you are still wet and the storm is still there. When you run to God, all the hurts and hard things might still be there—but God is with you, and things are better and can't hurt you so much. God helps His children with hard things. He makes them strong. Because He understands their hearts, they feel better. Because He is strong and good, they know they can trust Him.

But does a strong tower help if you don't run inside it? If you stay outside in the storm, you can't get the help or protection of the tower. You have to run inside the tower. And to get God's help and protection, we have to run to Him, too.

How does this work?

If you are sad because it is raining and you can't go to the zoo, what should you do? Pray and tell God how you feel—"El Roi, You are the God Who Sees.

You see the rain and my sadness. You understand. Thank You for understanding. I am Your servant, Adonai. You are the Lord. Whatever You do in my life is good and right. Help me to trust You."

If your math homework is really hard, run to El Shaddai—"God, You are El Shaddai, God Almighty. Nothing is too hard for You. You know all about math. Help me with my math problems. Help me to work hard and have a good attitude."

When strange noises at night scare you, remember that Jehovah-Shammah is with you—"Dear God, You are Jehovah-Shammah, the Lord Is There. You are always with your people. You are with me right now. Take away my fear and help me to trust You."

Sometimes change is hard. Families have new babies, friends move away, or Dad may need to travel, or we might lose a favorite teacher. But Yahweh never changes. Run to God. He is a Strong Tower—"Yahweh, everything changes. But not You. You are always the same. You are always strong, always loving, and always good. You are always a Strong Tower. Make me strong, too."

When you can't figure something out, run to Elohim, Strong Creator. He made everything! He never runs out of ideas. When you aren't sure about something, ask Jehovah-El Emeth, the LORD God of Truth, to help you know what is right. Whatever your problem, you can run to God, your Strong Tower.

The name of the LORD is a strong tower;
the righteous man runs into it and is safe. (Proverbs 18:10)

"Righteous" is a big word. What does it mean? "Righteous" means you are "right" before God. It means your sins are forgiven. The only way to be forgiven and be "right" before God is to trust in what Jesus did for sinners on the cross. Jesus took away the sins of sinners who trust in Him and made them righteous—or "right" before God.

So only those who are trusting in Jesus—who love Him and believe that He has paid for their sins—can run to God to be safe. God is a Strong Tower *only* for His children. Are you His child? Do you want to know God who is a Strong Tower for His children?

LEARNING TO TRUST GOD

✢ Draw a strong tower. Write Proverbs 18:10 on it. What are some of God's names? What does it mean to "run to God"? What does it mean to be "safe"?

✢ With your family, think of problems a person might have. How could that person "run to God"? How could God be a Strong Tower to that person?

✢ *Activity:* Find a big, strong tower. Go inside. How does the outside world seem to you when you are in the tower? Why is the tower a safe place? What could it protect you from? Why is God an even better Strong Tower?

Jehovah-Sabaoth
(jĕ **hō** vŭ să bā **ŏt**)
The Lord of Hosts

All the men in Saul's army were afraid of Goliath. He was a giant, big and strong, and he was mean. No one wanted to fight Goliath. No one except a boy named David.

David wasn't afraid. He was angry! Angry that Goliath would make fun of the armies of God! Angry that a giant with a sword looked so big to God's people. Angry that God's name was treated badly.

So David the boy faced Goliath the giant with these words:

You come to me with a sword and with a spear and with a javelin, but I come to you in the name of the Lord of hosts, the God of the armies of Israel, whom you have defied. (1 Samuel 17:45)

David saw the big giant and his strong army . . . but he also saw something even bigger. David saw the bigness of God, who is bigger than any giant, stronger than any enemy, greater than any army.

David knew that God is Jehovah-Sabaoth, the Lord of Hosts. A "host" is an army. El Shaddai, God Almighty, has "hosts" of angels—armies and armies of angels—that He can send to fight for His people and for His great name!

Angels are messengers. They tell people God's news, like "Jesus is born!," "Abram, your wife will have a baby!," and "Joseph, go to Egypt with Mary and Jesus."

But angels are also fighters. They are big, strong, fierce warriors! They fight for the living God. They do what He tells them to do. And God has thousands and thousands and thousands of angel warriors! God is Jehovah-Sabaoth, the LORD of Hosts.

Jehovah-Sabaoth, the LORD of armies and armies and armies of mighty angels, sends His mighty angels to help His people:

> For he will command his angels concerning you
> to guard you in all your ways. (Psalm 91:11)

David knew that Jehovah-Sabaoth is stronger than any giant or army. So did the prophet Elisha.

The king of Syria was very angry at Elisha. So he sent horses, chariots, and a big army to get Elisha. The great army of the king circled the whole city where Elisha was. The army came at night and waited for Elisha.

When Elisha's servant got up in the morning, what did he see? He saw the BIG army, around the WHOLE city. There was no way out. How do you think he felt?

He felt like anyone else who sees only big armies—he felt afraid!

Elisha saw the army, too. But he also saw something else. He saw that God is El Shaddai, God Almighty; El Elyon, the Most High, who is higher than any king; El Roi, the God Who Sees His people wherever they are; and Jehovah-Shammah, who was right there with him!

Elisha saw more than the army of the king. He saw the armies of Jehovah-Sabaoth, the LORD of hosts.

He said, "Do not be afraid, for those who are with us are more than those who are with them." Then Elisha prayed and said, "O LORD, please open his eyes that he may see." So the LORD opened the eyes of the young man, and he saw, and behold, the mountain was full of horses and chariots of fire all around Elisha. (2 Kings 6:16–17)

Jehovah-Sabaoth sent His mighty warrior angels to protect Elisha. Elisha knew that God is the LORD of armies of angels, and Elisha ran to his Strong Tower, Jehovah-Sabaoth.

And when the Syrians came down against him, Elisha prayed to the LORD and said, "Please strike this people with blindness." So he struck them with blindness in accordance with the prayer of Elisha. (2 Kings 6:18)

The blind army of the king could not hurt Elisha because Jehovah-Sabaoth was with him. Jehovah-Sabaoth is always with His people. His mighty angels "guard [them] in all [their] ways."

We can see and think about all the big, scary, sad, and hard things. Or we can see and think about Jehovah-Sabaoth. It takes faith to see God as big and other things as little. It takes believing that God is Jehovah-Sabaoth.

LEARNING TO TRUST GOD

✦ Read about Jehovah-Sabaoth in 1 Samuel 17 and 2 Kings 6:8–23.

✦ What do you think the army of God looked like to Elisha? Try to remember that God has His army around His people. Talk with your family about what God's army might be protecting your family from. Thank God for being Jehovah-Sabaoth.

✦ *Activity:* Ask your mom or dad to make a word-search[1] puzzle with God's names in it. Then find God's names—do you see them? Pray for faith to see God for who He is.

1. Check on the Internet for sites that will help you make word-search puzzles.

Jehovah-Jireh (jě hō vŭ jī rŭ)
The LORD Will Provide

What would you pack if you were going on a trip? Would you pack pajamas, a toothbrush, and shoes? Maybe you would, because we often know what we need.

But there are times when we don't know what we need. Suppose you found a caterpillar on your trip. You wouldn't have packed a jar for it because finding the caterpillar was a surprise. We can't know everything we are going to need.

But God always knows what we need. He knows what we need today . . . and what we *will* need tomorrow or next week. He knows about everything we will *ever* need. That's because El Roi, the God Who Sees, sees everything—everything now and everything for all our lives. So He never forgets what we are going to need, as we sometimes do when we pack for a trip.

What Bible stories show that God knows and takes care of what His children need?

God is Jehovah-Jireh, the LORD Will Provide. That means God "takes care of the needs" of His children. He gives them what He knows they need . . . and even what they *don't know* they need.

Before Jesus died on the cross to pay for sin, God's people used to ask His forgiveness for their sins by making sacrifices. They had to kill certain animals and burn them.

Abraham and his son Isaac went to make a sacrifice. They brought wood, a knife, and fire with them. What was missing?

They needed a sacrifice,[1] and Isaac knew this.

---

1. Because of the focus of this chapter, God's testing of Abraham by asking him to sacrifice Isaac is not mentioned here. You may want to read the story from Genesis 22:1–19 and explain the whole story to your child.

He said, "Behold, the fire and the wood, but where is the lamb for a burnt offering?" (Genesis 22:7)

Abraham, too, knew they needed a sacrifice. He also knew that God is Jehovah-Jireh, the LORD Will Provide.

Abraham said, "God will provide for himself the lamb for a burnt offering, my son." (Genesis 22:8)

Abraham was ready to make the sacrifice. But only Isaac was there. Abraham did not have a lamb, a goat, or even a dove. What would happen?

And Abraham lifted up his eyes and looked, and behold, behind him was a ram, caught in a thicket by his horns. (Genesis 22:13)

God gave Abraham a ram for the sacrifice because He is Jehovah-Jireh, the LORD Will Provide. So Abraham killed the ram and sacrificed it to ask God's forgiveness for sin. Is this the only sacrifice Abraham made?

No, Abraham and the people of Israel made many, many, many sacrifices, because they kept on sinning. What they really needed was a forever sacrifice—one that would pay for all the sins they did, and all the sins they *would* do the next day, and the next week, and all their lives.

God knew this. And God who is Jehovah-Jireh did give a forever sacrifice—His Son, Jesus, who died on the cross.

If God has given the very BEST, His VERY OWN SON, can He be trusted to give His children everything else they need? Yes, He can. That is why we can call Him Jehovah-Jireh, the LORD Will Provide.

God takes care of His children in a very special way, and He also provides for those who don't even love Him. What does this tell you about God?

How has God taken care of you? Let's thank God for being Jehovah-Jireh.

LEARNING TO TRUST GOD

✤ Read some Bible stories that show God provides for His children (for example, Exodus 17:1–7; 1 Kings 17:1–16; John 6:1–14). Does God give us everything we *want* or all that we *need*? God gives His children everything that is good for them. Read and talk about Romans 8:32.

✤ Ask your mom or dad to tell about a time when God showed He is Jehovah-Jireh by providing for them. Is there anything your family needs now? Can you trust Jehovah-Jireh to provide it, or something better?

✤ *Activity:* Sometimes God provides for others by sending us to help them. Does your family know of someone with a need? You could help an older person, or make a meal for a family with a new baby, or send a care package to a missionary, or encourage someone who is lonely.

Jehovah-Or (jĕ hō vŭ or)
The LORD Is Light

There are many ways to use the word "light." Have you heard the saying, "As light as a feather"? What does "light" mean there?

Right, it means "not heavy." But if you say that something is *light* blue, you don't mean that it's not heavy, do you? No, you mean that it's not dark. A light is also something you turn on when it is dark—it gives brightness to everything.

In the Bible, "light" sometimes means "goodness" or "without sin." And "darkness" means "evil" or "sinfulness." This is what John meant when he said:

This is the message we have heard from him and proclaim to you, that God is light, and in him is no darkness at all. (1 John 1:5)

"God is light" means God is full of goodness and holiness. There is no evil or sin in God. It is such a happy thing that God is good—all the time, every single part of Him.

But people aren't like this, are they? They are not full of goodness. There is sin and evil in everyone's heart. This is what John said about people:

And this is the judgment: the light has come into the world, and people loved the darkness rather than the light because their works were evil. (John 3:19)

People love the dark evil of Satan, more than the bright light of God's goodness. Lying, being mean, and thinking angry thoughts are easier for people than doing what is right and being loving. That is why we all need Jesus to give us new hearts—so that we love the light of His goodness, and hate the darkness of sin and evil. There is a story in the Bible that shows us about God's light of goodness and man's darkness of sin.

David, the king of Israel, stole another man's wife, Bathsheba, and treated her like his own wife. That was very wrong—it was a dark, evil sin. And David knew it was wrong. Instead of running to the Lᴏʀᴅ, his Strong Tower, and telling God about his sin, David tried to hide his sin. In hiding his dark, evil sin, David

sinned again by having Bathsheba's husband killed. Now there was even more dark, evil sin in his heart.

David thought his sin was hidden. But he was wrong. El Roi, the God Who Sees, saw David's sin, and He saw David's way of hiding his sin. He saw the dark evil in David's heart. God loved David so much that He would not let David live in the darkness of his sin.

So God, who is Jehovah-Or, the LORD Is Light, shined His light on David's dark sin and dark heart. God sent Nathan, a prophet, to tell David a story about a man who stole another man's sheep. When David saw the ugly, evil darkness of the man's sin, he was very angry!

But Nathan looked at David and said, "You are the man!" Jehovah-Or, the LORD Is Light, had shown David the dark evil of David's own sinful heart.

This time, David ran to the LORD, his Strong Tower. He admitted his sin and asked God to forgive him. He turned away from hiding his sin, and he walked away from doing evil.

Jehovah-Or, the LORD Is Light, shines His light into the dark evil of our hearts. He shows us His goodness and gives us a love for the light. If you have come to Jesus and asked Him to forgive your sins, and give you a new heart that loves the light of His goodness and hates evil, then you can sing with David:

The LORD is my light and my salvation. (Psalm 27:1)

✠ Read the story of Jehovah-Or in 2 Samuel 11:1–12:25. Where do you see in this story that God is Jehovah-Or, the LORD Is Light? What else do you see about God in this story?

✠ Read Matthew 5:14–16. If God is light, how can men also be called light? How can good works show others that God is Jehovah-Or?

✠ *Activity:* How can you and your family show others that God is Jehovah-Or? With your family, do a "good work" and pray that the person you bless will see God as Jehovah-Or.

Jehovah-Shalom
(jĕ hō vŭ shä lōm)
The LORD Is Peace

The Israelites were scared of their enemies—they were so afraid that they hid in caves. They were scared because the Midianites were strong and stole their food and animals.

Why would Jehovah-Sabaoth, the LORD of Hosts, with his armies and armies of angels, let this happen to Israel?

God is not only Jehovah-Sabaoth, the LORD of Hosts, He is also El Kana, Jealous God. Yahweh, the God of Israel, said the people must worship Him alone. They must not worship other, false gods such as Baal and Asherah. But the Israelites did not obey God. They built altars to make sacrifices to Baal and put up worship poles for Asherah.

So God let their enemies steal their food and animals. He let the Israelites be afraid and live in caves. They were not at peace—they had worry and fear in their hearts and were fighting with their enemies. God let them have more and more trouble so that they would turn away from other gods and call to Him.

When things got really, really bad, the Israelites cried out to God, their Strong Tower. He heard them and sent a prophet to tell them about their sin of disobeying God and worshiping other gods. He also sent an angel to tell a farmer named Gideon:

Go in this might of yours and save Israel from the hand of Midian; do not I send you? (Judges 6:14).

Was Gideon excited? No, he was still scared.

And he said to him, "Please, Lord, how can I save Israel? Behold, my clan is the weakest in Manasseh, and I am the least in my father's house." And the LORD said to him, "But I will be with you, and you shall strike the Midianites as one man." (Judges 6:15–16)

Jehovah-Shammah, the LORD Is There, promised to help. But Gideon still wasn't sure. Maybe if God showed him that He was really God and that He was strong, then Gideon would have peace in his heart—without worry and fear. Maybe then the Israelites could be at peace with their enemies without fighting.

So Gideon brought an offering of meat and bread to God. The angel reached out his stick to touch them, and God burned up the offering! Then Gideon knew God was really with him. Gideon felt God's peace—that gentle, sweet feeling of not being afraid or worried. He knew Israel would have peace, and God would stop the fighting with Midian. So Gideon built an altar to God, Jehovah-Shalom, the LORD Is Peace.

That night God told Gideon to pull down the altar of Baal and the worship pole of Asherah. Gideon obeyed God, and then built an altar to Yahweh, the One True God, El Kana, who will not share His people's love and worship with another god.

But this is not the end of the story of Gideon, the Midianites, and Jehovah-Shalom. God helped the Israelites defeat their enemies—not with a big army of 22,000, or even 10,000, but with a very small army of only 300 men! The army was small, but God is BIG! He is El Shaddai, God Almighty!

Jehovah-Shalom gave Israel peace with its enemies. The LORD Is Peace.

God gives other kinds of peace, too. He gives His children the gentle peace in their hearts of not worrying or being afraid. But His children must "run" to Him, their Strong Tower. They must trust Him—believe He is big, strong, good, and wise.

> You keep him in perfect peace
>   whose mind is stayed on you,
>   because he trusts in you. (Isaiah 26:3)

But there is an even better kind of peace that Jehovah-Shalom gives—peace with God. Every single person is born fighting against God—as His enemy. Everyone wants his own way, not God's way. Only Jehovah-Shalom can change that.

Jehovah-Shalom made peace with man through the death of His Son, Jesus, on the cross. When you trust in Jesus as your Savior, God takes away your fighting heart and gives you a new heart of peace with Him. Jesus died on the cross so that you could have peace with God.

But he was wounded for our transgressions;
    he was crushed for our iniquities;
upon him was the chastisement that brought us peace,
    and with his stripes we are healed. (Isaiah 53:5)

LEARNING TO TRUST GOD

✦ Read about Jehovah-Shalom in Judges 6–8. Why does God punish His people? What can you learn about God in this story?

✦ Read Isaiah 53:5. Ask your mom or dad for help with the big words. Rewrite the verse in your own words. Thank Jesus for dying to make peace between God and man, and confess any disobedience to God.

✦ *Activity:* How is peace broken between us and others? Is there anyone you need to make peace with? If so, what should you do? Will you do it now? Ask your mom or dad to share a peace-making story.

Judge of the Whole Earth

Imagine two pieces of candy—a candy bar and a lollipop—and two children who both want the lollipop. Their father must decide who gets the lollipop. He is like a "judge." He decides. He says the way it will be. He says "yes" to one child and "no" to the other.

Real judges usually sit behind a big desk and make important decisions. They decide whether a person did something wrong and what the punishment will be. What the judge decides is the way it is. The person can't change what the judge says, because the judge is in charge.

El Elyon, the Most High, is a judge, too. He is not just the judge of a city or even a country. He is the Judge of the Whole Earth. That means He is the judge of every single person in every city, in every country of the whole world, every person—big, small, young, old, boy, girl, man, and woman.

Someday, Jesus will come back again, and then God will do His judging. The Judge of the Whole Earth will sit on a "great white throne," and will open a very important book called the Book of Life. Why is it called the Book of Life?

This book has the names of everyone who will have life—who will live forever in heaven with God. To enter heaven, you must be perfectly right in God's eyes.

And if anyone's name was not found written in the book of life, he was thrown into the lake of fire. (Revelation 20:15)

The lake of fire will be more awful than we can imagine. And it will be forever. Everyone will be judged. Every person will stand before the great white throne to face the Judge of the Whole Earth. Everyone will go to either heaven or hell.

God will bring every deed into judgment, with every secret thing, whether good or evil. (Ecclesiastes 12:14)

Just think of it. Everything you have ever done will be told. Every good thing you have done will be told—such as being kind or forgiving, or telling the truth. And every bad thing you have done will be told—being mean or angry, or taking something that isn't yours. Nothing you have ever done will be forgotten or missed. El Roi, the God Who Sees, knows it all.

You would be "guilty," which means you have sinned and deserve to be punished forever. That would be the most frightening, awful thing.

BUT if you have trusted Jesus as your Savior, if you are a child of God, Jesus has already paid for your sin. We don't know exactly how things will happen, but perhaps Jesus will say something like, "He trusts in me, and I paid for his sin on the cross. I have given him my perfect sinlessness."

God's judgment will be:

There is therefore now no condemnation for those who are in Christ Jesus. (Romans 8:1)

There will not be ANY PUNISHMENT for those who have trusted Jesus! No punishment AT ALL—even though we deserve it. Although we have sinned many times, there will be no punishment because Jesus has already taken our punishment on the cross.

There will be great rejoicing—joy and laughter and singing! This will go on forever and ever and ever! There will be no more tears, sickness, pain, sadness, or death . . . only joy with Jesus and all His people forever and ever!

No one will ever be able to change the judgment of the Judge of the Whole Earth, because He is El Elyon, the Most High. He is Yahweh who is Unchanging, who will always keep His promises. He is Jehovah-El Emeth, the LORD God of Truth, who cannot lie and has said that there is no punishment for those who trust in Jesus.

✤ What will heaven be like? Read Revelation 21:1–22:5. What will hell be like? Read Matthew 13:40–43. Why is Jesus' death on the cross good news for sinners?

✤ Memorize Romans 8:1. You could even make up a song with the words and sing it.

✤ *Activity:* Add any missing names to your poster of God's names. Do you know someone who isn't trusting in Jesus? What name of God could you share with that person? Pray for that person and then, with your mom or dad, tell that person about God's name. You may want to bring a Bible or another book about God as a gift.

Jehovah-Maginnenu
(jĕ hō vŭ mä gĭ nĕ new)
The Lord Our Defense

Have you ever had a water balloon fight or a snowball fight? Was it fun? How did you protect yourself? You could run away, or dodge the balloon or snowball. You could find something to hide behind, or use something to block the attack—like a shield. What could you use as a shield?

A shield protects or "defends" us from being hit. Without a shield, a lot more snowballs or water balloons would hit us!

Did you know that God is also a shield? The Bible says:

You are my hiding place and my shield. (Psalm 119:114)

Our soul waits for the Lord;
    he is our help and our shield. (Psalm 33:20)

God is like a shield, standing in the way of things that would hurt His children. He blocks us from attack. He is Jehovah-Maginnenu, the Lord Our Defense.

God was Jehovah-Maginnenu when Moses was attacked—not with snowballs, but with something that hurts even more . . . with unkind words. This attack of words came from Moses' own sister and brother, Miriam and Aaron. They didn't like Moses' wife, and they didn't like that Moses was in charge of the people of Israel.

And they said, "Has the Lord indeed spoken only through Moses? Has he not spoken through us also?" And the Lord heard it. (Numbers 12:2)

What did Jehovah-Maginnenu do? He defended Moses! God had chosen Moses to be the leader of His people. God had spoken to Moses, and Moses had led the people just as God told him. So God was angry when Miriam and Aaron complained about Moses. He was so angry that He told Miriam and Aaron they were wrong, and punished them for their sin.

God was a shield standing in the way of the attacks against Moses. He is Jehovah-Maginnenu, the LORD Our Defense.

But that doesn't mean we won't get hurt sometimes. The Bible says, "Our soul waits for the LORD." Sometimes God lets His children "get hit" a few times before He stands in the way of the attack. He helps His children be strong in the attack, and when the time is right He defends them.

God waited to defend Jesus. Many people did not believe Jesus is the Son of God. They were angry and wanted Jesus killed. They brought Him to Pontius Pilate to decide whether Jesus would be killed, and said many untrue things about Jesus. But Jesus did not defend Himself from the lies. He knew that His Father, Jehovah-Maginnenu, would defend Him.

He committed no sin, neither was deceit found in his mouth. When he was reviled, he did not revile in return; when he suffered, he did not threaten, but continued entrusting himself to him who judges justly. (1 Peter 2:22–23)

Do you know what happened then? Pilate let Barabbas go, a wicked, evil murderer, and sent Jesus, who never did anything wrong, to be killed. What happened? Did God forget to be Jehovah-Maginnenu and defend Jesus? Did El Roi not see what was happening? Was El Shaddai not strong enough to protect Jesus?

Jehovah-Maginnenu, the LORD Our Defense, let the people kill Jesus. He let them think Jesus was not the Son of God. Then He raised Jesus from the dead and PROVED that Jesus is His Son! He defended Jesus by showing the people that nothing could hurt Jesus forever. Nothing could win over Jesus in the end.

Do you know why God let Jesus die on the cross? Do you know why He waited to defend Jesus? So that Jehovah-Maginnenu could protect us from the punishment we deserve because of our sin. Just like Miriam and Aaron, we have all sinned and need to be protected from God's anger at sin. And GOD HIMSELF has been our defense! He is Jehovah-Maginnenu, the LORD Our Defense!

He himself bore our sins in his body on the tree, that we might die to sin and live to righteousness. By his wounds you have been healed. (1 Peter 2:24)

LEARNING TO TRUST GOD

✤ Read about Jehovah-Maginnenu in Numbers 12:1–16. How serious is sin? Why do we all deserve to be punished? How have you sinned? How can you trust in Jehovah-Maginnenu to be your shield?

✤ God is a hiding place—a place of safety and protection. What do you need protection from? How does God protect you through your parents? How does God protect you through His Word? Thank God for being Jehovah-Maginnenu, the Lord Our Defense.

✤ *Activity:* Have a friendly family fight with snowballs, water balloons, or wadded paper balls! Be sure to have a shield. Then talk about how God is a shield for His people.

Jehovah-Rohi (jĕ hō vŭ rō hē)
The Lord My Shepherd

Do lions need people to take care of them? How about monkeys, whales, snakes, or eagles? They don't, do they? God has made these animals so that they can take care of themselves.

But sheep are different. Most sheep need someone—a shepherd—to take care of them. Sheep aren't very smart, and they get scared easily. They don't have sharp teeth and can't climb trees, so they can't protect themselves. That is why they need a shepherd.

A good shepherd takes care of his sheep with tender love. He has oil to put on their cuts and to keep bugs away. Because sheep are easily scared, he plays music on his flute or harp to make them feel safe.

How did shepherds in Bible times protect their sheep? They carried clubs—like big bats—to beat away thieves and wild animals. Sometimes they used a "sling" like the one David used to throw stones at wild animals.

A shepherd also carried a "staff" or a "crook"—a long stick with a hook on the end. What is a staff used for?

Sometimes the shepherd uses the staff to dig out poisonous plants from the field so that the sheep won't eat them and become sick. He also uses it to push thornbushes out of the way so that the sheep won't get scratched. When the sheep don't know where to go, the shepherd guides them with the staff—pointing the way and grabbing sheep that start to wander away. If a sheep falls into a tight spot, the shepherd can pull it up with the hook on the end of the staff.

When we see sheep, most of them look the same to us. But a shepherd knows every one of his sheep and calls them by name. Each one is important to him.

God wants us to understand that He tenderly loves and cares for His children. Each one is important to Him. So in the Bible He tells us they are like sheep, and He is like a shepherd to them.

Know that the LORD, he is God!
It is he who made us, and we are his;
we are his people, and the sheep of his pasture. (Psalm 100:3)

Just as a shepherd protects and cares for his sheep, God protects and cares for His children. He comforts them when they are afraid or hurt. He shows them the right way, and He pulls them back when they try to wander away from Him and from what is right and good. When they fall into sin, He picks them up and puts them back on the good and right path. He is loving and kind. And best of all, God cares for each of His children and knows them by name.

If you are trusting Jesus as your Savior, even though there are billions and billions of people in the world, God knows your very name . . . because He is Jehovah-Rohi, the LORD My Shepherd.

David was a shepherd who loved God very much. He would often sing songs about God while watching his sheep. David was a shepherd, but he also was a sheep of Jehovah-Rohi, the LORD My Shepherd. This is one of the songs David sang about Jehovah-Rohi:

The LORD is my shepherd; I shall not want.
    He makes me lie down in green pastures.
He leads me beside still waters.
    He restores my soul.
He leads me in paths of righteousness
    for his name's sake.

Even though I walk through the valley of the shadow of death,
    I will fear no evil,
for you are with me;
    your rod and your staff,
    they comfort me.

You prepare a table before me
    in the presence of my enemies;

you anoint my head with oil;
    my cup overflows.
Surely goodness and mercy shall follow me
    all the days of my life,
and I shall dwell in the house of the LORD
    forever. (Psalm 23:1–6)

LEARNING TO TRUST GOD

✢ Read the parable of the lost sheep in Luke 15:3–7. What is the meaning of this story?

✢ Memorize some of Psalm 23.

✢ *Activity:* Learn what you can about sheep and shepherds. Make a booklet telling how God is like a shepherd and His people are like sheep. Look at pictures of sheep. Can you tell them all apart? Would you know each one's name? Thank God for knowing and caring for each of His children.

Father

Jesus told a story that is both sad and happy. Sad *and* happy? How can it be both? Let's see.

A father had two sons. The younger was disobedient and did not like his father's rules. So he asked his father for some money, and left home. Now he could do whatever he wanted. But what he wanted wasn't good. It wasn't good at all. He spent all his money doing the wrong things. Then he had no money for food, so he got a job feeding pigs. This is the sad part of the story.

One day, the son thought to himself, "I'm starving! But my father's servants have plenty to eat." So he made a decision—a good decision.

> I will arise and go to my father, and I will say to him, "Father, I have sinned against heaven and before you. I am no longer worthy to be called your son. Treat me as one of your hired servants." (Luke 15:18–19)

So he started home, and when he got close his father saw him. What did his father do? Was he angry? Did he tell the son to go away again?

No, his father was full of kindness and forgiveness. He ran and hugged and kissed his son! He told his servants to bring the best robe and nice shoes, and have a big celebration! This is the happy part of the story.

But the older son wasn't happy. He didn't want a party for his disobedient brother! He was angry that his father forgave the younger son, because he did not realize that he was a sinner, too. He was full of pride—he thought he was better than he really was. He thought the party should be for him!

Do you know why Jesus told this story? He told it so that we could know what God the Father is like.

God is Elohim, Strong Creator. He made everything, so it all belongs to Him. Just like the father in the story, He is generous. He shares His world and everything in it with us. He is El Elyon, the Most High, and all His ways are good and right. To turn against His ways is wrong and disobedient, and is sin.

God is El Roi, the God Who Sees with kindness. He is Jehovah-Shalom, who wants to make peace even with disobedient sons. So Jehovah-Maginnenu gave His very own Son to be our defense against His anger at sin. God is a loving Father

who wants to welcome disobedient children and celebrate with them—and this is the very, very happy part of the story.

Jesus also told the story so that we would know what we are like. We are like the two sons. We are disobedient and ungrateful. We have forgotten to thank God for His goodness. We have broken His commands, and need His forgiveness. We think we are good, but we are sinners who need God.

But there is still another reason Jesus told this story. He told it so that His Father could be our Father, too. Jesus came to earth to die on the cross so that we could have the very best, most loving, forgiving Father—so that we could be children of God!

But to all who did receive him, who believed in his name, he gave the right to become children of God. (John 1:12)

God is not everyone's Father. But He has promised to be Father to all who welcome Jesus' payment for our sin, and believe in His name—for all who believe that God is who He says He is, and trust that God will be all that He tells us He is, in His many, many names, through Jesus His Son. God wants to be your loving Father. But you must believe and trust that He is:

Elohim, Strong Creator
Yahweh, Self-Existent, Unchanging
El Shaddai, God Almighty
El Elyon, the Most High
El Kana, Jealous God
Jehovah-El Emeth, the Lord God of Truth
Adonai, Lord
El Roi, the God Who Sees
Jehovah-Shammah, the Lord Is There
A Strong Tower
Jehovah-Sabaoth, the Lord of Hosts

Jehovah-Jireh, the LORD Will Provide

Jehovah-Or, the LORD Is Light

Jehovah-Shalom, the LORD Is Peace

Judge of the Whole Earth

Jehovah-Maginnenu, the LORD Our Defense

Jehovah-Rohi, the LORD my shepherd

You can have a warm friendship with God and call Him "Abba, Father." You can be a child of God through faith in Jesus.

LEARNING TO TRUST GOD

✛ Read the story Jesus told to show us what kind of father God is (Luke 15:11–32). How are you like the two sons? How is God like the father? What kind of father is God?

✛ What does "Like father, like son" mean? How are God's children like their heavenly Father?

✛ *Activity:* With your mom or dad, make a flag or a kite. Write on it the names of God you have learned. Talk about how you can "believe in God's name" as you work together. Then fly your flag or kite.

Lamb of God, Savior

He was just a baby—a little boy born to Mary. What should Mary and Joseph name Him? That was easy because an angel had already told them:

> You shall call his name Jesus, for he will save his people from their sins. (Matthew 1:21)

His name was easy. What was hard was His job: "he will save his people from their sins." Such a little baby and such a big, *impossible* job.

For hundreds and hundreds of years, God's people made animal sacrifices to pay for their sins. Thousands and thousands of animals were killed—bulls, sheep, goats, doves, and pigeons. They were perfect animals, and their blood was the payment for sin.

> Without the shedding of blood there is no forgiveness of sin. (Hebrews 9:22)

The people had to sacrifice again and again and again.

What could this little baby do? Surely He couldn't save His people from sin, could He?

But the message came again. This time it came to shepherds watching their sheep:

And the angel said to them, "Fear not, for behold, I bring you good news of great joy that will be for all the people. For unto you is born this day in the city of David a Savior, who is Christ the Lord." (Luke 2:10–11)

A Savior is someone who comes to "save" God's people from their sins. Was baby Jesus the Savior? How could one person take the punishment for the sins of all of God's people?

Jesus grew up and became a man. Was He the Savior? Once more the message came. This time it came from His cousin, John the Baptist.

He saw Jesus coming toward him, and said, "Behold, the Lamb of God, who takes away the sin of the world." (John 1:29)

The Lamb of God? Lambs had been used to pay for sins for hundreds of years. They were just lambs from the field, but with no scratches or problems—perfect lambs. But John called Jesus the Lamb of *God*. So Jesus is the Lamb sent from God to His people to pay for their sins.

Jesus is even more than that. His many names tell us that He is more than the baby of Mary, now a grown man. Remember that in the Bible names have meanings. Have you ever heard names like these?

Master
Immanuel—God with Us
Light of the World

Prince of Peace
Overcomer
The Way, the Truth, and the Life
The Good Shepherd

Jesus was not only the baby of Mary—He is also the Son of God! His names are like God's names!

The Way, the Truth, the Life—Jehovah-El Emeth, the LORD God of Truth
Master—Adonai, Lord
Immanuel, God with Us—Jehovah-Shammah, the LORD Is There
Light of the World—Jehovah-Or, the LORD Is Light
Prince of Peace—Jehovah-Shalom, the LORD Is Peace
Overcomer—Jehovah-Sabaoth, the LORD of Hosts
The Good Shepherd—Jehovah-Rohi, the LORD My Shepherd

Jesus' names are like God's names because Jesus is God! Everything that God is, Jesus is.

So Jesus was the perfect, without-sin Lamb of God, who was killed on a cross for the sins of God's people. Because He is God, He did not stay dead but rose to be the living Lamb of God. God's living sacrifice, His very own perfect Son, is the once-and-for-all, forever sacrifice for sin.

But as it is, he has appeared once for all at the end of the ages to put away sin by the sacrifice of himself. (Hebrews 9:26)

Mary and Joseph knew who Jesus really is. So did John the Baptist. Do you? Is He your Savior? Are you trusting Him as God's perfect Lamb of God to pay for your sins?

LEARNING TO TRUST GOD

✤ Read about the crucifixion and resurrection of Jesus in Mark 15 and 16. Why is "Lamb of God" a good name for Jesus?

✤ Read Isaiah 53:5–6. Find the meanings of the big words in these verses. Why is Jesus the Prince of Peace?

✤ *Activity:* Talk about the names of Jesus with your mom or dad as you write them on your poster. Tell someone one of Jesus' names and explain how Jesus is like that name.

Messiah, Christ

How does someone become president of the United States? People choose him by voting. In a special ceremony, he promises to defend the laws, protect the country, and do his job well.

Can he do this by himself? No, he has helpers, called Cabinet members. It is a great honor and an important job to be a Cabinet member. The only way to be one is to be chosen by the president.

In the Old Testament, certain people were chosen for the high honor of important jobs, too. But they weren't chosen by a president or a king. They were chosen by *God*! There was a special ceremony in which oil was poured on their heads. This was called "anointing" with oil. It showed that God had chosen them specially for a high position and an important job.

In the Bible, three kinds of people were anointed with oil—prophets, priests, and kings. Can you think of someone who was a prophet?

Prophets were special messengers of God, telling the people His very words. They told the people to follow God, and warned them of their sin. Sometimes they told about things that would happen in the future. Can you think of a prophet who was God's messenger? What happened?

When the people sinned, they could not go directly to God for forgiveness. They needed someone to take their sins to God. Priests made sacrifices to God for the people to ask His forgiveness for their sin. They also prayed for the people. Can you think of a priest in the Bible?

Kings ruled the people. They were in charge and had great power. Who were some of God's anointed kings of Israel?

All these people were anointed by God—chosen by Him for the high honor of a special job. But there was one person—one most important, most special, most honored person—chosen by God to be a Prophet *and* a Priest *and* a King! He was called the "Anointed One" or the Messiah.

God promised to send this most special Prophet, Priest, and King, who was greater than all the rest. The people waited for hundreds of years for the Messiah to come. They were taken captive by their enemies, and the temple was destroyed, but still the Messiah King did not come. Even when they returned to Israel to rebuild the temple, the Messiah did not come. They still waited.

They waited through the rule of the army of Alexander the Great, and the Greeks . . . and the great overthrow of Greek rule by the Maccabees. Now that they ruled themselves, surely the Anointed One would come. But still the Messiah did not come. Had God forgotten His promise?

Finally, they were conquered by the Romans. Living under Roman rule was hard. The people looked for the Messiah King. They thought He would come with great power as a warrior king, who would free them from the Romans and set up His kingdom.

During the time of the Romans, a baby was born in a stable. His birth was announced to shepherds by an angel:

Fear not, for behold, I bring you good news of great joy that will be for all the people. For unto you is born this day in the city of David a Savior, who is Christ the Lord. (Luke 2:10–11)

Suddenly the sky was filled with angels praising God.

Wise men from the East came looking for the child, saying:

Where is he who has been born king of the Jews? For we saw his star when it rose and have come to worship him. (Matthew 2:2)

Why would they worship Him? Was this the Anointed One? Was this the promised Messiah?

The angels called Him the Savior, Christ the Lord. Could Christ be the Anointed One, the Messiah? The word for "Messiah" or "Anointed One" in the Greek language is "Christ." The angels knew who this child was. He was the Savior, Christ the Lord, the Messiah promised by God, who always keeps His promises.

God's promised Prophet and Priest and King had come! There should be great rejoicing by the people, who had waited so long for the Messiah! . . . But there wasn't.

Only a few people rejoiced and believed that Jesus was the Messiah. But most people wondered how a baby born in a stable, a carpenter from Galilee, could be the Messiah. He wasn't rich or powerful. He didn't have a big army. They were looking for a big, strong, powerful king to fight the Romans. They couldn't see that Jesus was the Messiah, because they were looking for the wrong kind of Messiah.

Jesus said, "My kingdom is not of this world" (John 18:36).

Jesus did not come as a warrior king. His kingdom was a spiritual kingdom. He came as a Prophet, Priest, and King. How is Jesus a Prophet? How is He a Priest? And how is He a King?

Jesus was the Prophet who told people that He was the way to God. He told them about God's kingdom where the humble are honored, enemies are forgiven, and real treasures are forever treasures in heaven.

Jesus is the Priest who paid the price for the sins of His people by sacrificing Himself on the cross. He rose and lives in heaven, where He prays for His people.

And Jesus is the King who came as a servant, washing His disciples' feet, healing the blind, and loving the poor. He is the King waiting in heaven until His Father sends Him back as a powerful, ruling King, who will squash all His enemies under His majestic feet.

Jesus is the Christ, the Messiah, the Anointed One, the Savior of the World. Not everyone believes this. Do you?

Now when Jesus came into the district of Caesarea Philippi, he asked his disciples, "Who do people say that the Son of Man is?" And they said, "Some say John the Baptist, others say Elijah, and others Jeremiah or one of the prophets." He said to them, "But who do you say that I am?" Simon Peter replied, "You are the Christ, the Son of the living God." And Jesus answered him, "Blessed are you, Simon Bar-Jonah! For flesh and blood has not revealed this to you, but my Father who is in heaven." (Matthew 16:13–17)

LEARNING TO TRUST GOD

✢ Read about Simon Peter's seeing Jesus as the Anointed One in Matthew 16:13–17. How did Peter know who Jesus is? Why didn't others know this? How can you know Christ?

✢ Read John 10:22–31. What are the two kinds of people in this story? How do you become part of Jesus' flock? Why then is prayer so important? Pray for those you know who are not part of Jesus' flock.

✢ *Activity:* Watch an inauguration or a coronation ceremony. What responsibilities does this person have? As the Prophet, Priest, and King, what are Jesus' responsibilities? Has He failed in any of them? Is He still a Prophet, Priest, and King? How?

Salvation in No Other Name

Suppose, while playing outside, you touch some poisonous weeds. Later, your hands itch and have red bumps. Your problem gets worse each day, so your mother brings you to the doctor. The doctor checks your hands and says, "I see you have a problem. This medicine will take away your problem. Just rub it on the spots two times a day."

But you say, "I don't think I like that medicine. I am just going to rub grape jelly on my hands. I like grape jelly better." Do you think the grape jelly would take care of the problem? No. You can't just make up your own way to take care of your problem. You must use the right medicine. You have to trust the doctor.

You may not have itchy bumps on your hands, but you do have a problem—a very serious problem. That problem is sin, and there is only one way to fix it. El Elyon, the Most High, made one way to fix the sin problem. It is Jesus, the Lamb of God.

And there is salvation in no one else, for there is no other name under heaven given among men by which we must be saved. (Acts 4:12)

Because God is the Most High, He has the right to decide the way to be saved from sin. He is wise, and Jehovah-El Emeth always tells the truth. He has said that Jesus is the only way to be saved from the punishment for sin. To fix the sin problem, you have to trust God. Only Jesus can change sinful hearts.

Zacchaeus was a rich man. He was a tax collector, and his job was to take the tax money from people. But he took more money than he was supposed to take. He kept some of it for himself, and became rich. He was greedy and unfair, and he lied.

Most people did not like Zacchaeus. But Jesus did. Jesus loved Zacchaeus even though Zacchaeus was a sinner.

When Jesus visited Zacchaeus's town, what do you think He did? He looked right at Zacchaeus, who was sitting in a tree, and said:

Zacchaeus, hurry and come down, for I must stay at your house today. (Luke 19:5)

Most people didn't want to be around Zacchaeus. But Jesus wanted to visit with him. Zacchaeus welcomed Jesus. He was so glad Jesus wanted to come to his house. He could see that Jesus loved him.

After visiting with Jesus, Zacchaeus wanted to give back not just the money he wrongly took but even *more* money. Being with Jesus changed Zacchaeus's heart. Only Jesus can change sinful hearts. Only Jesus can fix the sin problem.

Many people were angry that Jesus loved sinful people.

And the Pharisees and their scribes grumbled at his disciples, saying, "Why do you eat and drink with tax collectors and sinners?" And Jesus answered them, "Those who are well have no need of a physician, but those who are sick. I have not come to call the righteous but sinners to repentance." (Luke 5:30–32)

The Lamb of God came so that sinners could have peace with God. Jesus came to give God's forgiveness to anyone who would believe that He is God's perfect Lamb and trust Him for forgiveness of sin. Anyone who welcomes Jesus can be saved—even people like Zacchaeus. Even sinners like you and me.

For "everyone who calls on the name of the Lord will be saved" (Romans 10:13). This means everyone, even sinners like the thief on the cross who believed in Jesus. Can you think of other sinful people in the Bible who trusted Jesus for salvation? *Everyone* who calls on the name of the Lord will be saved!

✤ Read the story of another tax collector in Luke 5:27–32. Who are sinners? What does "repentance" mean?

✤ Pray for those who do not admit that they are sinners and are not trusting in Jesus for forgiveness. Make a prayer list and keep praying for these people.

✤ *Activity:* With your family, think of a way that you can tell the good news about forgiveness for sin. Pray for God's help in telling the story about Jesus' taking the punishment for sinners, and then do it.

Helper

Jesus left heaven to be born as a baby, and then grow up to die for the sins of His people. But earth wasn't His real home. Heaven is His home. So after Jesus rose from the dead, He went home to heaven.

Jesus knew the disciples would miss Him. He knew His children would need to remember what He taught them. He knew all Christians everywhere would need help to fight sin. He knew sinful people would need to understand that they are sinners.

He also knew His Father had a good and wise plan for the world and His people. God the Father, who sent the Son to die, would also send God the Holy Spirit to help His people.

> But the Helper, the Holy Spirit, whom the Father will send in my name, he will teach you all things and bring to your remembrance all that I have said to you. (John 14:26)

Jesus promised that the Helper, the Holy Spirit, would come to help His people understand about God and His right way of living. His people need the Holy Spirit's help to tell other people about Jesus. Even though His people were sad that Jesus was going away, Jesus knew God's plan was good.

> Nevertheless, I tell you the truth: it is to your advantage that I go away, for if I do not go away, the Helper will not come to you. But if I go, I will send him to you. And when he comes, he will convict the world concerning sin and righteousness and judgment. (John 16:7–8)

Jesus had to go back to heaven so that He too could send the Holy Spirit. The Holy Spirit would show people that they were sinners, and help them understand

God's way of fixing the sin problem. Jesus told the disciples to wait for the Holy Spirit in the city of Jerusalem.

So the disciples waited. And as God promised, the Helper came. They heard *a sound like a mighty rushing wind*, and the Holy Spirit came with power. The Helper, who helps people understand about Jesus and sin, gave the disciples words in different languages. There were people from many countries in Jerusalem, and every person heard about Jesus in his own language!

At first the people were confused. What was going on?

But Peter stood and started preaching. He told them that the Helper, the Holy Spirit, had come. He told them that *everyone who calls on the name of the Lord will be saved.* And he told them about Jesus, whom God had sent . . . and whom they had killed.

Peter also told them the good news that Jesus rose from the dead! Peter preached, and the Helper did the work God had sent Him to do. As Peter preached, the Holy Spirit helped the people understand they were sinners.

"Brothers, what shall we do?" they asked.

What do you think Peter told them? What would you say if someone asked you what to do about sin?

Peter told them to "repent"—to turn away from their sin of not trusting Jesus. God would forgive their sins and give them the Holy Spirit.

For the promise is for you and for your children and for all who are far off, everyone whom the Lord our God calls to himself. (Acts 2:39)

The people turned from their sin. They put their trust in Jesus. They received God's forgiveness, and believed God's promise. The Holy Spirit came with mighty power for Peter to preach, and for the people to turn from sin. And 3,000 people believed in Jesus that day!

The promise to give the Holy Spirit is for all Christians everywhere. If you trust and love Jesus and want to obey Him, the Holy Spirit will help you. The Helper will help you understand the Bible.

When you do something wrong, and you know in your heart that it's wrong, maybe that's the Holy Spirit helping you. He helps you understand that sin is wrong and ugly, and that God doesn't like it. Listen to the Helper and turn away from sin. The Holy Spirit can show that you need Jesus.

LEARNING TO TRUST GOD

✤ Read the story of the Holy Spirit's coming in Acts 2. Ask God to send the Holy Spirit to help you understand the Bible and trust in Jesus.

✤ Is the Helper showing you any sin in your life? What should you do about sin? Ask God to give you a heart to turn away from sin.

✤ *Activity:* Make a booklet to explain the good news about Jesus. Include pictures and verses. Pray for God's help, and use your booklet to tell someone about Jesus. Trust the Holy Spirit to work in that person's heart.

Coming King

How can you tell whether someone is a king?

Usually kings live in palaces and have many servants. They wear robes and crowns, and sit on big thrones. They make laws, and punish people who break these laws. They are in charge, and usually have a lot of money. When the king comes, people cheer and bow down to him.

But it wasn't that way for Jesus.

Jesus is the most important king. He is the King of Kings, who made the whole world, and rules everything and everyone.

He was in the world, and the world was made through him, yet the world did not know him. He came to his own, and his own people did not receive him. (John 1:10–11)

Jesus came into His world, but most people did not know He was a king. He didn't look like a king. He didn't wear a robe or crown. He was born in a stable, not in a palace. Most of the time, He didn't even have a home.

He didn't have any servants. In fact, He served others. Once people cheered and bowed down to Him, but only for a short time. Then they killed Him on a cross. That was the only time He wore a crown. But it was a crown of thorns, not a crown with jewels. And instead of cheering for Him then, people made fun of Him.

Jesus didn't seem like a king because:

Though he was in the form of God, [he] did not count equality with God a thing to be grasped, but made himself nothing, taking the form of a servant, being born in the likeness of men. (Philippians 2:6–7)

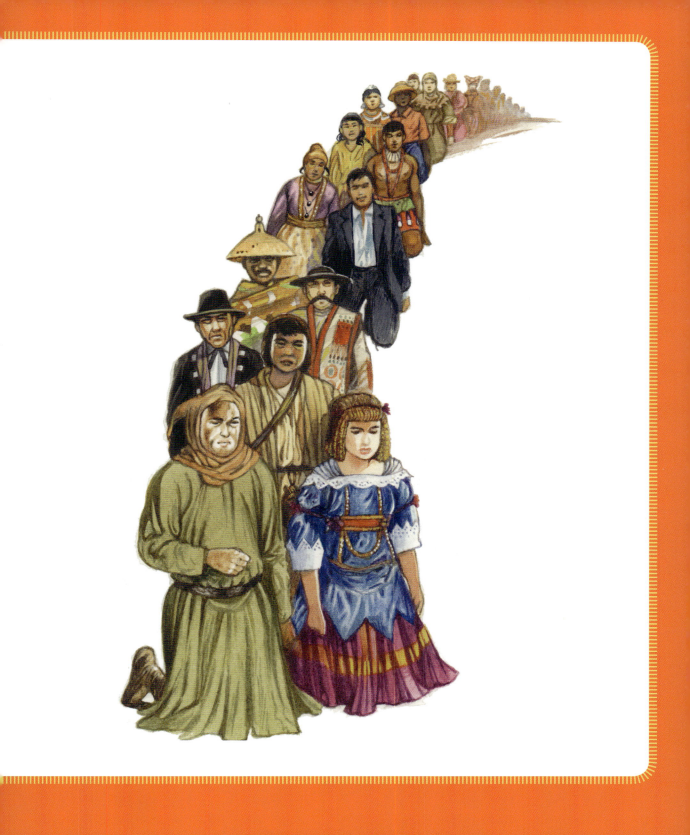

Jesus is God, but He left heaven and came as a man to serve others. So Jesus didn't seem like a king, and He wasn't treated like a king.

But He is a king, and someday the *whole world* will know it! Someday Jesus will come back to earth. But this time He will come as a king, not as a baby! He will come as the King of Kings riding a white horse! This time He will be wearing a robe and many crowns.

The armies of heaven—all the angel armies of Jehovah-Sabaoth, the LORD of Hosts—will follow Him. What a mighty parade that will be! Trumpets will sound, and all the people who have died and love Jesus will rise from the dead to meet Him. They have been waiting for the Coming King!

For the Lord himself will descend from heaven with a cry of command, with the voice of an archangel, and with the sound of the trumpet of God. And the dead in Christ will rise first. (1 Thessalonians 4:16)

Everyone in the world will know this is King Jesus! His name will be greater than any other name—King Jesus, the Coming King, is the King of Kings!

At the name of Jesus every knee should bow, in heaven and on earth and under the earth, and every tongue confess that Jesus Christ is Lord, to the glory of God the Father. (Philippians 2:10–11)

This time everyone will know Jesus is a king. They will know Jesus is the Greatest King who ever lived, the King of All Kings. This time they will "receive" Him. Every person in every country of the world, young and old, will bow down to King Jesus. Even those who don't want Jesus to be king will bow, because no one will be able to turn away from Him this time. King Jesus is the Coming King and the King of Kings forever and ever.

Are you waiting for Jesus the Coming King? Do you pray for Him to come back?

Come, Lord Jesus! (Revelation 22:20)

LEARNING TO TRUST GOD

✢ Read John 1:1–13. Some people did not welcome Jesus. How does a person turn away from Jesus today? Others did welcome Jesus. What does the Bible say about them? How does a person become a child of God?

✢ Sing songs about the Coming King.

✢ *Activity:* The Bible says King Jesus has saved people from every tongue, tribe, and nation. Look at a world map and see all the countries. Learn something about people from another country or countries. Cook one of their recipes or play one of their games. Then pray for them.

Overcomer

Soldiers must be trained so that they can fight well. They must work hard and do everything they are told. One way they train is with an obstacle course. Do you know what an obstacle is?

An obstacle is something that gets in the way and slows you down or makes it hard for you to go somewhere. It can be a tunnel to go through, a low fence to crawl under, a net or rope to climb, something to jump over, or bars to cross on your hands. A soldier must be able to beat or "overcome" every obstacle and finish the course quickly.

An overcomer is someone who sees obstacles and does not stop. An overcomer defeats or wins over every obstacle.

When Jesus returns as the Coming King, He will also show the whole world that He is the Overcomer. What obstacles will Jesus win over or defeat?

Before Jesus comes, there will be great suffering or "tribulation." There will be earthquakes, wars, and famines—times when there isn't much food. God's enemies will be powerful and rule on earth. There will be much evil, and it will seem that Satan is winning against God. But this is all part of God's plan and Jesus' return as Coming King and Overcomer.

Immediately after the tribulation of those days the sun will be darkened, and the moon will not give its light, and the stars will fall from heaven, and the powers of the heavens will be shaken. Then will appear in heaven the sign of the Son of Man, and then all the tribes of the earth will mourn, and they will see the Son of Man coming on the clouds of heaven with power and great glory. And he will send out his angels with a loud trumpet call, and they will gather his elect from the four winds, from one end of heaven to the other. (Matthew 24:29–31)

God could crush all His enemies right now, but He is waiting patiently, giving people time to turn from sin. But someday God will crush His enemies. Jesus will come with great power to get His children and defeat evil, Satan, and all of God's enemies. God's enemies will fight, but they will not win.

They will make war on the Lamb, and the Lamb will conquer them, for he is Lord of lords and King of kings, and those with him are called and chosen and faithful. (Revelation 17:14)

Jesus will not stop until every enemy has been beaten, every evil squashed. He will throw Satan and all of God's enemies into hell, and bring His children home to heaven. This will be a great day for God's children—and a horrible day for those who do not trust in Jesus.

You are either an enemy of God or a child of God. You are either on God's side or on Satan's. There are no other sides.

How can you tell that you are a child of God? This is what the Bible says:

And by this we know that we have come to know him, if we keep his commandments. Whoever says "I know him" but does not keep his commandments is a liar, and the truth is not in him, but whoever keeps his word, in him truly the love of God is perfected. By this we may know that we are in him: whoever says he abides in him ought to walk in the same way in which he walked. (1 John 2:3–6)

If you love God, you will love what is right. Your heart will want to obey. You will *walk in the same way* Jesus walked—forgiving others, loving unlovely people like Zacchaeus, telling others about God's goodness and greatness.

If your heart doesn't want to follow God's commands, you do not love God. But Jesus the Overcomer will overcome your hard heart if you turn to Him and ask Him.

If you love God and trust Jesus each day, Jesus the Overcomer will help you fight sin in your own heart. He will help you overcome evil in the world. There are many evils, but here is good news for you from the Bible:

Little children, you are from God and have overcome them, for he who is in you is greater than he who is in the world. (1 John 4:4)

Jesus is greater than all—He is El Shaddai, God Almighty. He is El Elyon, the Most High. Jesus is the great Overcomer who will overcome all evil!

LEARNING TO TRUST GOD

✢ Read about the "sheep" and "goats" in the final judgment in Matthew 25:31–46. What does verse 40 mean? What is the reward for sheep and punishment for goats?

✢ We can't even imagine Jesus' return. We have never seen anything so powerful, glorious, or terrible. How do you think it might be? What would a reporter say about it?

✢ *Activity:* With your family, set up an obstacle course and see how fast you can go through it. Remember that Jesus the Overcomer will someday overcome everything that stands against Him.

Knowing God's Name and Trusting Him

You have learned a lot of names for God. How many of them can you remember?

Elohim: Strong Creator

Yahweh: Self-Existent, Unchanging

El Shaddai: God Almighty

El Elyon: The Most High

El Kana: Jealous God

Jehovah-El Emeth: The LORD God of Truth

Adonai: Lord

El Roi: The God Who Sees

Jehovah-Shammah: The LORD Is There

A Strong Tower

Jehovah-Sabaoth: The LORD of Hosts

Jehovah-Jireh: The LORD Will Provide

Jehovah-Or: The LORD Is Light

Jehovah-Shalom: The LORD Is Peace

Judge of the Whole Earth

Jehovah-Maginnenu: The LORD Our Defense

Jehovah-Rohi: The LORD My Shepherd

Father

Lamb of God, Savior

Messiah, Christ

Helper

Coming King

Overcomer

This is a long list of names. But these are just a few of the many, many names of God. God is so glorious, so wonderful that it takes *hundreds of names* to show what He is like.

God's names are more than just names. They tell us what God is like. So knowing God's names is a good way to understand who God is. And understanding who God is can help you trust Him.

And those who know your name put their trust in you,
    for you, O LORD, have not forsaken those who seek you. (Psalm 9:10)

God is always just what His names say He is. You can trust that. He never changes. But just knowing God's names doesn't make you a child of God. You can know all about God, but not love Him or His commands.

Saul was a leader in the Jewish church. He followed many of the rules of the church . . . but he didn't follow Jesus. He hated people who followed Jesus, and worked to have them put in prison or even killed. Saul knew *about* God, but he did not trust in Jesus, the Lamb of God.

Jesus did not hate Saul. While Saul was traveling to the town of Damascus, a bright light from heaven flashed around him.

And falling to the ground he heard a voice saying to him, "Saul, Saul, why are you persecuting me?" (Acts 9:4)

Who spoke to Saul? Saul wasn't sure.

And he said, "Who are you, Lord?" And he said, "I am Jesus, whom you are persecuting. But rise and enter the city, and you will be told what you are to do." (Acts 9:5–6)

It was Jesus, the Lamb of God who had died for Saul's sins. Saul knew *about* Jesus—he knew that Jesus had many followers, that He taught about God, and that He died on a cross. But now Saul *met* Jesus.

When Saul got up from the ground, he couldn't see. His eyes were open, but he was blind. He couldn't see trees, people, or the road. But now he could see something he couldn't see before—now he could see who Jesus truly is. Now he believed that Jesus is the Son of God.

Before, Saul knew *about* God; now He knew God as his Savior, his Light, and his Peace.

LEARNING TO TRUST GOD

✛ Read the story of Saul meeting Jesus in Acts 9:1–22. How can you tell that Saul was a changed person? How did Saul follow Jesus?

✛ Ask God to show you that He is like His names. Look for ways God shows who He is.

✛ *Activity:* Finish your poster of God's names. You might want to look up more names and add them to your poster. Then choose one name to explain to someone else. Ask your parents how they met Jesus.

children desiring God

This storybook was adapted from *How Majestic Is Your Name*, an upper-elementary Sunday school curriculum published by Children Desiring God. If you would like to further explore the names of God or other aspects of His counsel with your student, resources are available from Children Desiring God.

Children Desiring God is a nonprofit ministry that Sally Michael and her husband, David Michael, helped to establish in the late 1990s. CDG publishes God-centered, Bible-saturated, Christ-exalting resources to help parents and churches spiritually train their children in the hope that the next generation will see and embrace Jesus Christ as the One who saves and satisfies the soul. Resources include kindergarten through youth curriculum (see sequence chart below), parenting booklets, and Bible memory resources. Free parenting and Christian education training audio lectures are also available online.

Please contact us if we can partner with you for the joy of the next generation.

childrendesiringGOD.org • cdg@desiringGOD.org

	SUNDAY SCHOOL	MIDWEEK
K	**Jesus, What a Savior!** A Study for Children on Redemption	**He Has Been Clearly Seen** A Study for Children on Seeing and Delighting in God's Glory
1	**The ABCs of God** A Study for Children on the Greatness and Worth of God	**I Stand in Awe** A Study for Children on the Bible
2	**Faithful to All His Promises** A Study for Children on the Promises of God	(Children Desiring God will announce plans for this title in the future.)
3	**In the Beginning . . . Jesus** A Chronological Study for Children on Redemptive History	**The Way of the Wise** A Study for Children on Wisdom and Foolishness
4	**To Be Like Jesus** A Study for Children on Following Jesus	**I Will Build My Church** A Study for Children on the Church (future release)
5	**How Majestic Is Your Name** A Study for Children on the Names and Character of God	**Pour Out Your Heart before Him** A Study for Children on Prayer and Praise in the Psalms (future release)
6	**My Purpose Will Stand** A Study for Children on the Providence of God	**Fight the Good Fight** A Study for Children on Persevering in Faith
7	**Your Word Is Truth** A Study for Youth on Seeing All of Life through the Truth of Scripture	**Abiding in Jesus** A Study for Youth on Trusting Jesus and Encouraging Others
8	**Teach Me Your Way** A Study for Youth on Surrender to Jesus and Submission to His Way	**Rejoicing in God's Good Design** A Study for Youth on Biblical Manhood and Womanhood (future release)